Start Now in Pastel

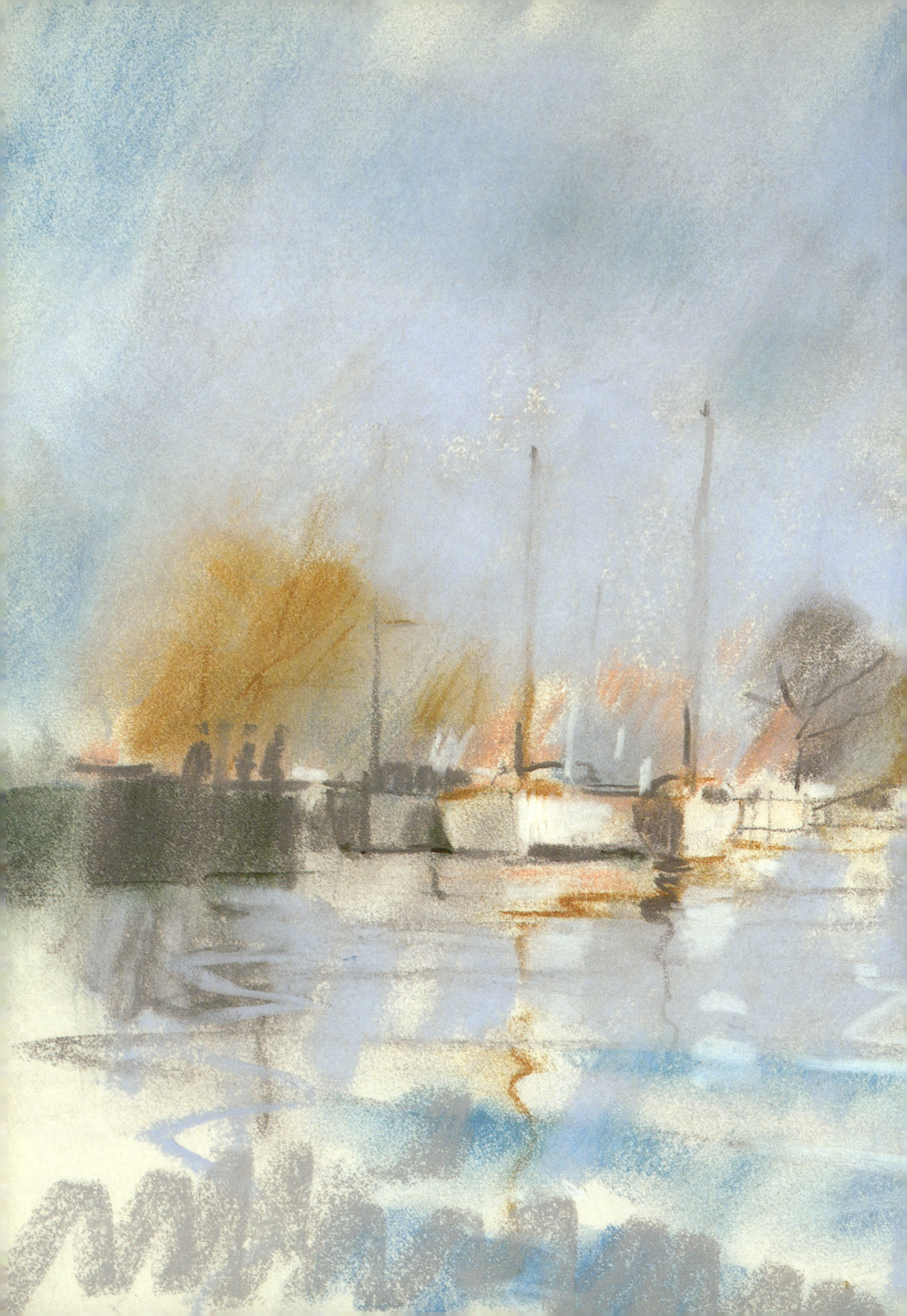

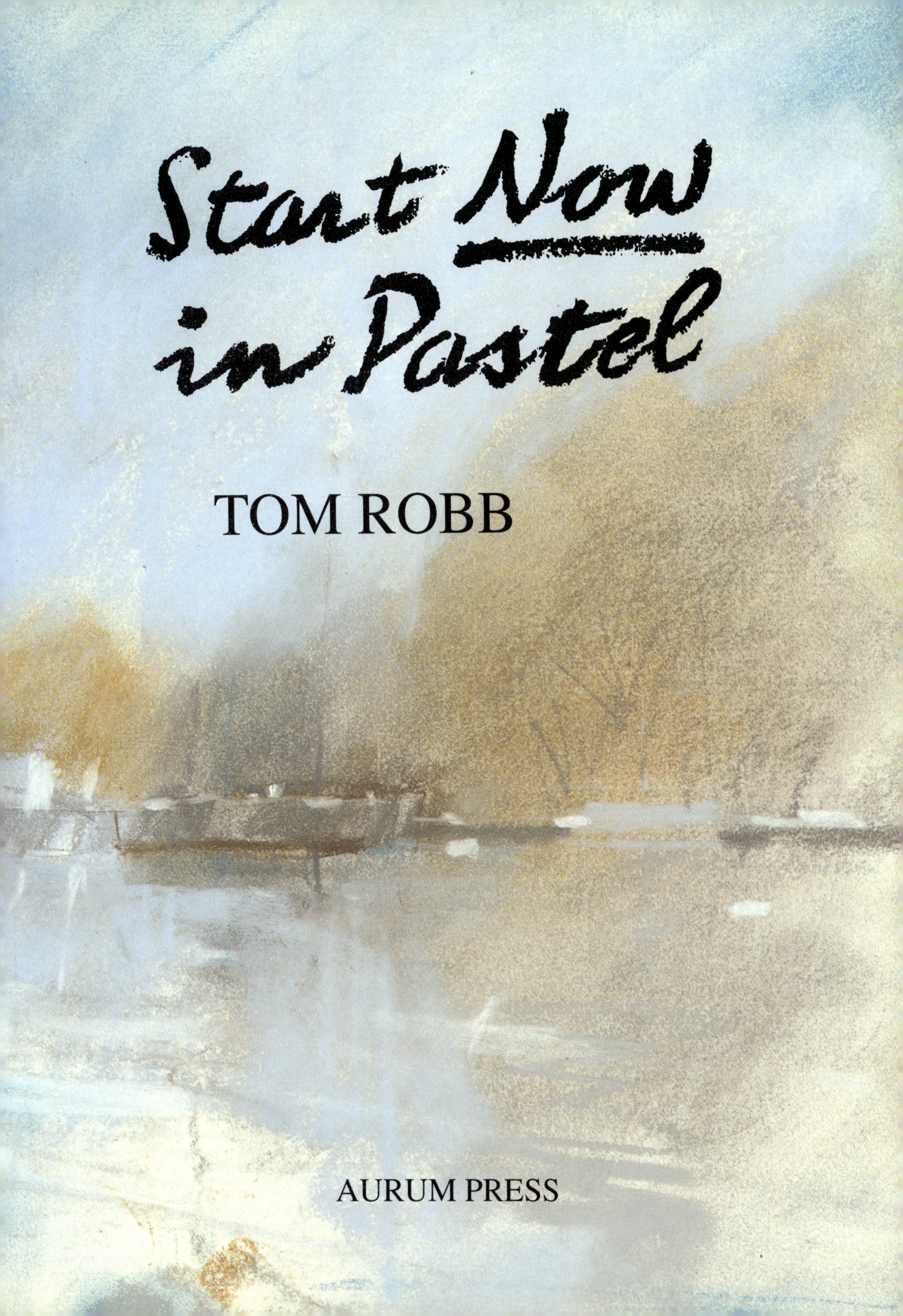

Start Now in Pastel

TOM ROBB

AURUM PRESS

First published 1993 by Aurum Press Ltd,
10 Museum Street, London WC1A 1JS

A catalogue record for this book is available from the British Library

ISBN 1 85410 241 9

10 9 8 7 6 5 4 3 2 1
1997 1996 1995 1994 1993

Printed in Belgium by Proost

Contents

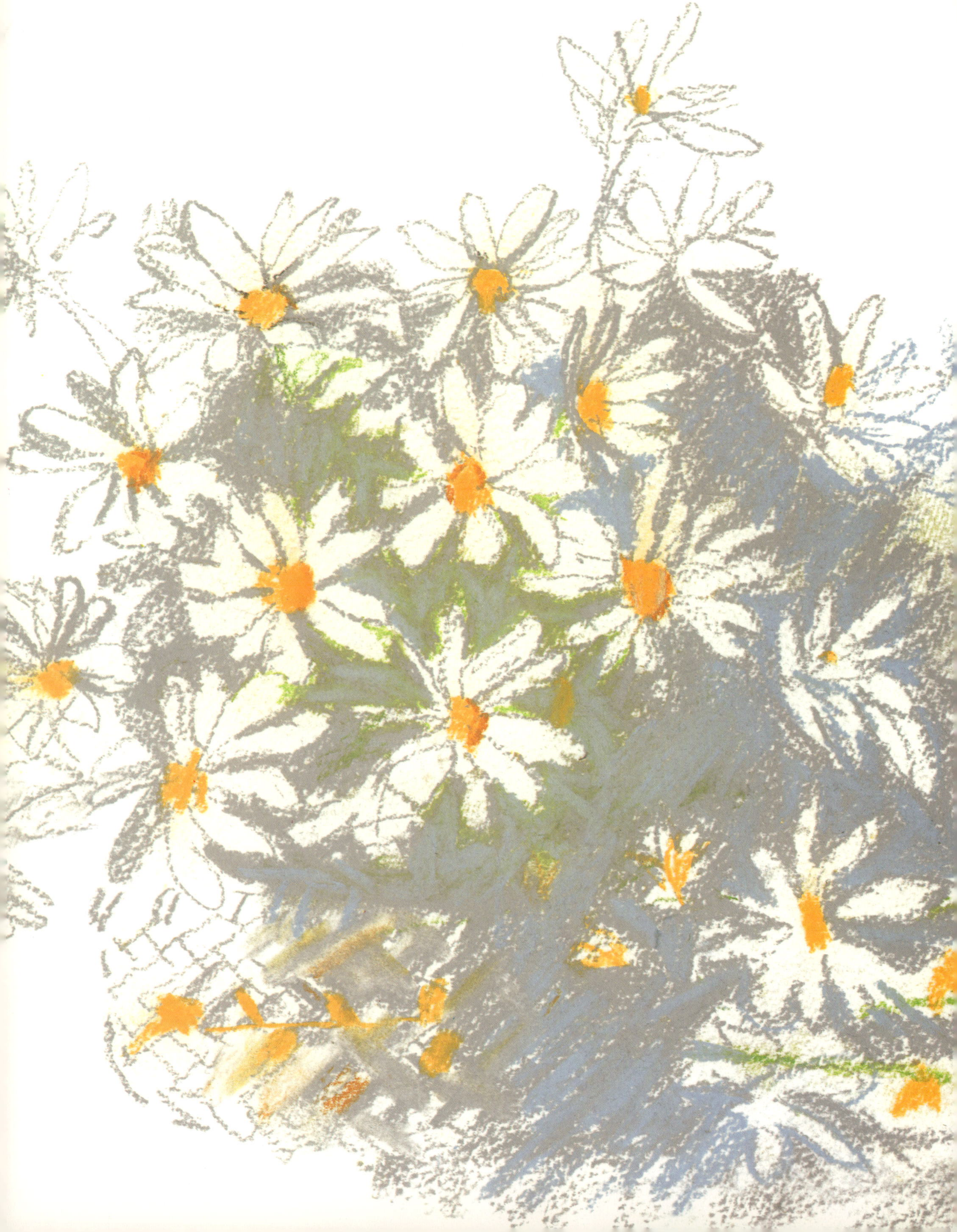

INTRODUCTION

Actually starting to draw or paint is the first hurdle any would-be artist faces. The idea comes easily to many people – on an afternoon's visit to a fine gallery, or a stroll past a painter working at an easel – and doing it yourself suddenly seems such a natural thing to try.

But all too often that is as far as it gets. Problems seem to rise up out of the ground – what kind of medium, what kind of subject, where to start? Even a visit to the art shop can offer so many choices that the original impulse fades rapidly.

Well, you can start now! Within a few pages you will be experimenting with all the fun of making pictures – pictures that you will be delighted to pin up and display as you progress through the thirty projects.

Pastels are particularly simple and direct to use, and offer immediate results. But once you have them in your hand you are in for a surprise. It is easy to imagine that the word 'pastel' still means only pinks, mauves, greys and pale blues, but the average range of traditional soft-stick pastels available today includes about 160 colours, and that's before you start blending or mixing them.

Textures have changed, too. The newer oil pastels, looking like thick, sticky, paper-wrapped crayons, are as shiny, bright and brilliant as any brush-and-oil medium. Though their range of colours is more limited, new versions include iridescents and even Day-Glo fluorescents.

An additional pleasure is that pastels are instantly responsive – light pressure gives light colour, heavier pressure gives a richer colour. What could be simpler?

So turn the page and start creating pictures, now!

Tom Robb
Phoebe Phillips (Editor)

PART ONE: STARTING NOW!

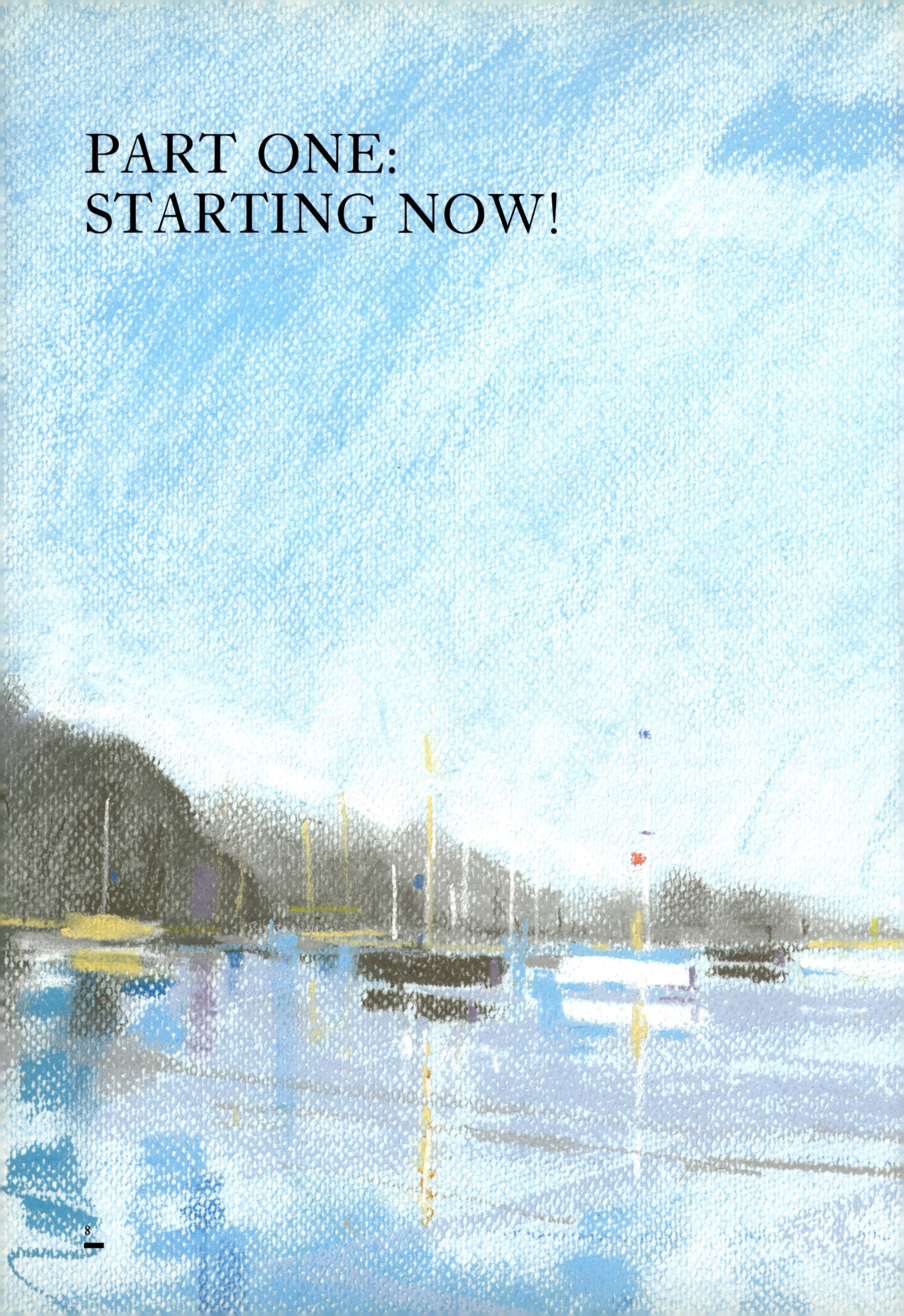

Every child crayons its way through colouring books without inhibition. Pastels have been called the adult crayon, and with good reason. They seem designed to help the artist begin to make wonderful drawings. The colours alone are so inviting that I defy you to stop, once you've picked up a stick and made tentative marks on the paper. And then you'll add a new colour, and another . . .

In these first three projects I want to make that invitation even more exciting. We'll cover the three fundamental techniques, as well as looking at the process of fixing, which keeps your drawing fresh. Since by their very nature pastels are fragile, you will need a simple spray fixative, and then your efforts will be perfectly preserved.

Because pastel dust floats in the air very easily, be sure to work on a sheet of light canvas or newspaper, so that when you blow off the excess it can easily be cleaned up later.

Most pastel drawings benefit in appearance from a simple cardboard mount. Make yourself a few, based on the size of the pad of paper you are using, and keep them handy to 'frame' the drawing before you decide you have finished. You will find full instructions for making mounts on p. 91, and advice on fixatives to buy on p. 92.

Be prepared: once you start drawing in pastels, you'll be hooked for a lifetime. Pin these first projects up on the wall to remind you how much pleasure is in store.

Delphiniums

This simple image is drawn with traditional, soft-stick pastels. To make a thin line, use a corner of the pastel; as that becomes flat use another corner, and so on. If the tip becomes too blunt, then break the stick gently. You will have two pieces and eight new corners!

The cluster of flowers on the head of a delphinium is very complicated. Simplify by using a scribbled line; work in figure-of-eight shapes, keeping your wrist relaxed and moving quickly down from the narrow top to the thicker base. As a guide you can make pencil marks around the space you want to fill.

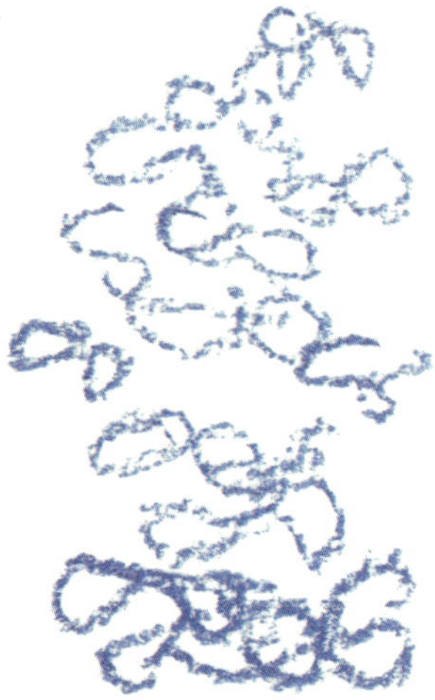

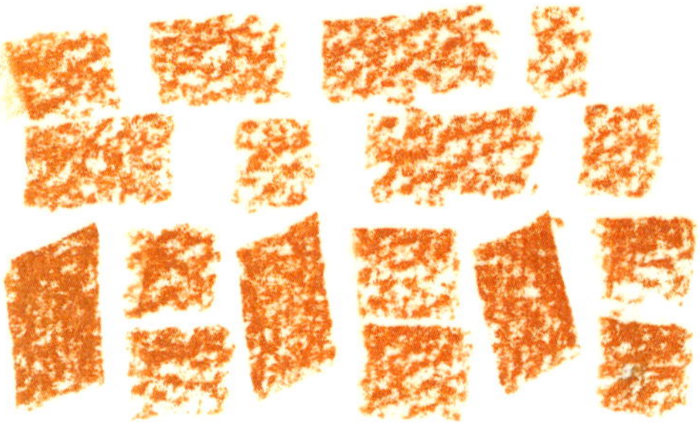

For the bricks you will need a small piece of pastel. Use the long side to give you a thick stroke. Hold the piece lightly – you won't need much pressure. Practise lifting the stick at intervals, making various lengths until you find a natural rhythm that resembles brickwork; remember to stagger the layers!

When you put it all together, work on the delphiniums first. Use different colours to give you depth: deeper, richer colours in front, paler colours at the back to recede. Add a few lines in green for the stems. Leave a gap of white around the flower-heads to let them stand out from their background.

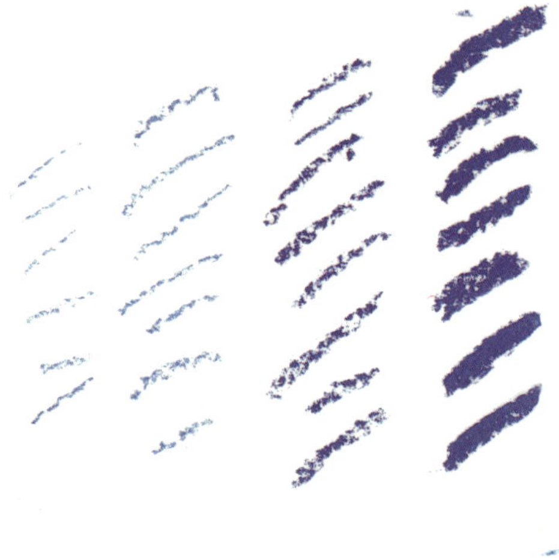

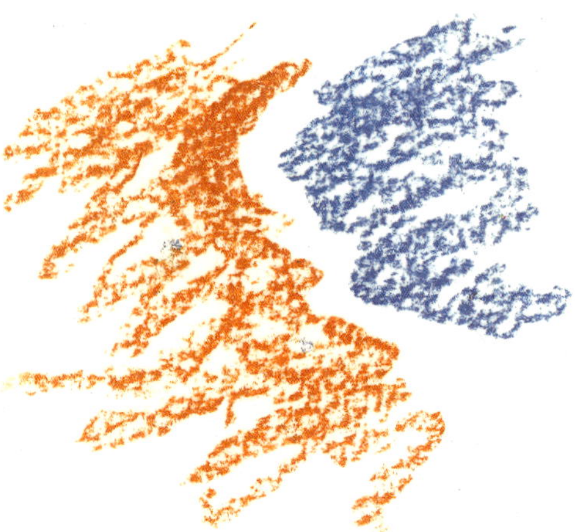

Pastel smudges very easily, so keep your fingers, wrists and arms off the paper as much as you can. If you do get the paper dirty, rub it clean with a good eraser.

As soon as you have finished, tilt the paper away from you, blow the surface lightly to remove any excess powder, and then spray the entire drawing immediately with a good fixative. Make sure you let it dry thoroughly.

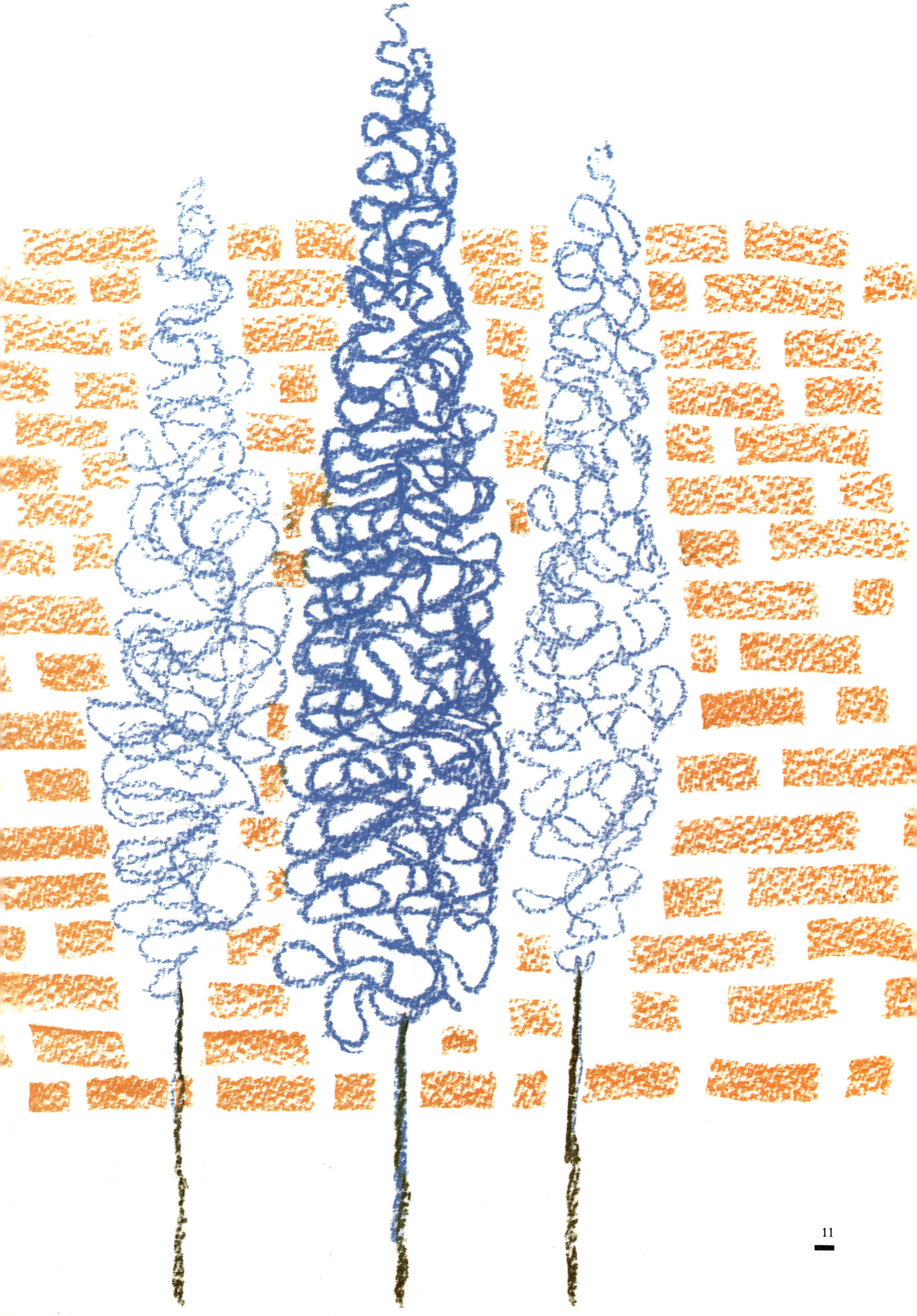

Pavilion in the Park

On this first project with oil pastels be prepared to get very dirty hands. The crayons are a combination of crumbliness and stickiness, and I often end up rubbing tiny bits over the paper to avoid wasting the colour.

Oil pastels are not easy to use in thin, delicate lines; simple blocks of colour make the best use of their incredibly rich texture.

Most parks have small buildings or pavilions scattered in the grounds. There are also plenty of advertisements and magazine articles to copy that feature garden buildings of all kinds.

Start by making shapes in the lighter colours. There are white pastels, both soft and oil, but if you are working on white paper, let the paper do some of the work. I also used the white paper to show the way sunlight was glittering on the edge of the grass. Against the other rich colours, it adds sparkle to a bright summer's day.

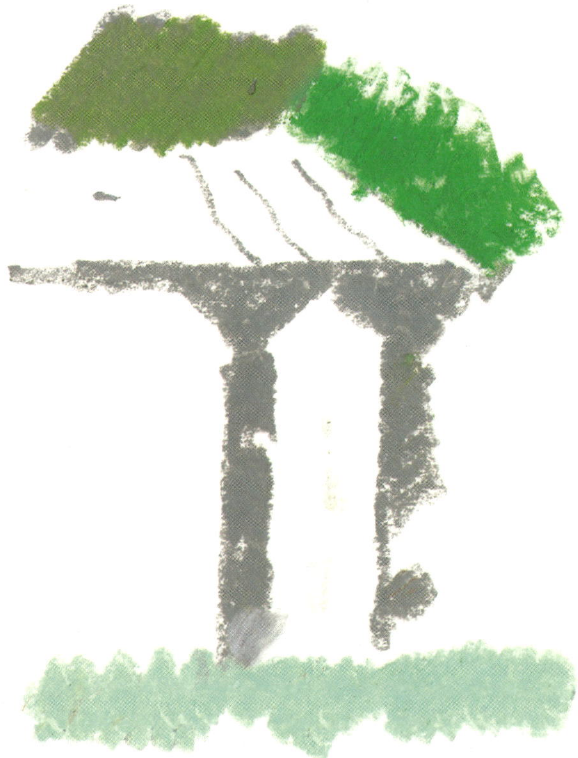

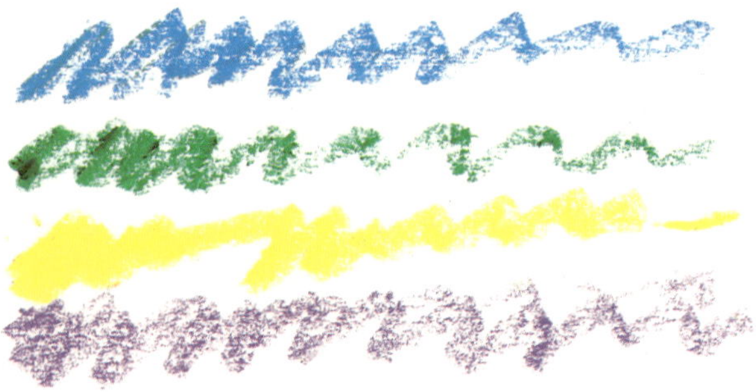

Experiment with seeing how much pressure you need to make lighter and heavier lines. Oil sticks react differently to soft pastels, and you will need to adjust the pressure when you change mediums, and even when you change brands.

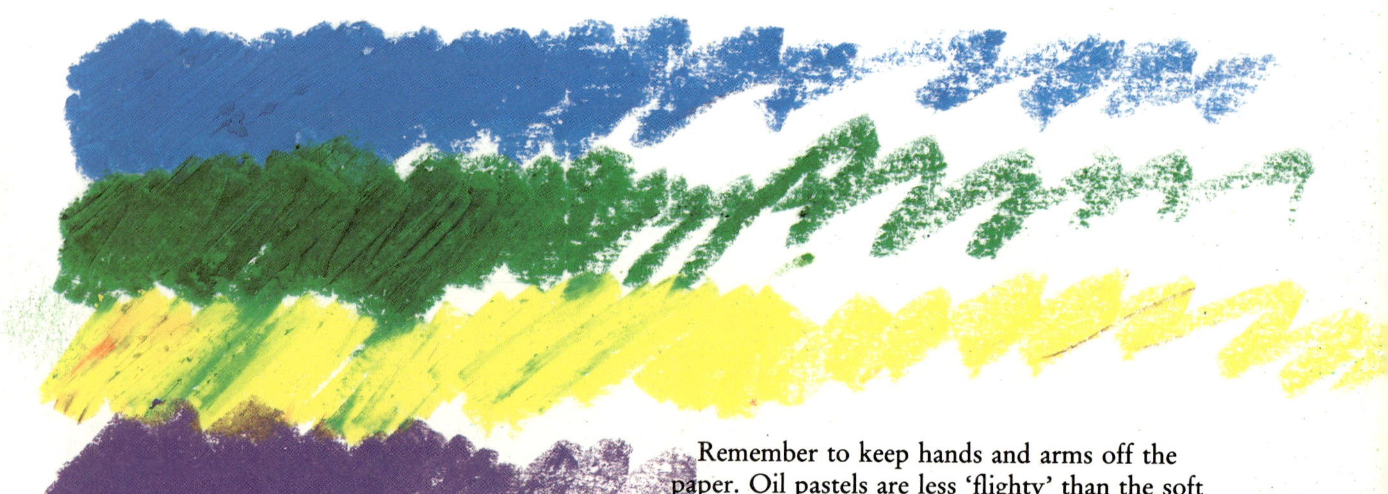

Remember to keep hands and arms off the paper. Oil pastels are less 'flighty' than the soft kind, but instead of floating in the air the specks cling to your skin.

Project 3 — First Studies

Landscape

In the first of these introductory studies you could see how delicate traditional pastels can be, especially when used in line and short, chunky pieces. Here we explore some of the more dramatic effects you can achieve using longer pieces of the sticks on their side.

Practise drawing long lines of pastel, using a stick 2 or 3 inches (5–7.5 cm) long. Hold it lightly along its length and sweep across the paper, making sure that the colour is as even as possible from right to left.

When you are happy with the result, take a fresh piece of paper and repeat the sweeps, but adding a little more pressure at one end of the stick (usually the end under your first finger is easiest). This will give you a graduated effect.

The first finger controls the darkest line, while the bottom finger can lift the stick away from the paper, adding an open texture and shape. Sweep right down the page in graduated colours, starting with the lightest at the top and moving down to the darkest at the bottom.

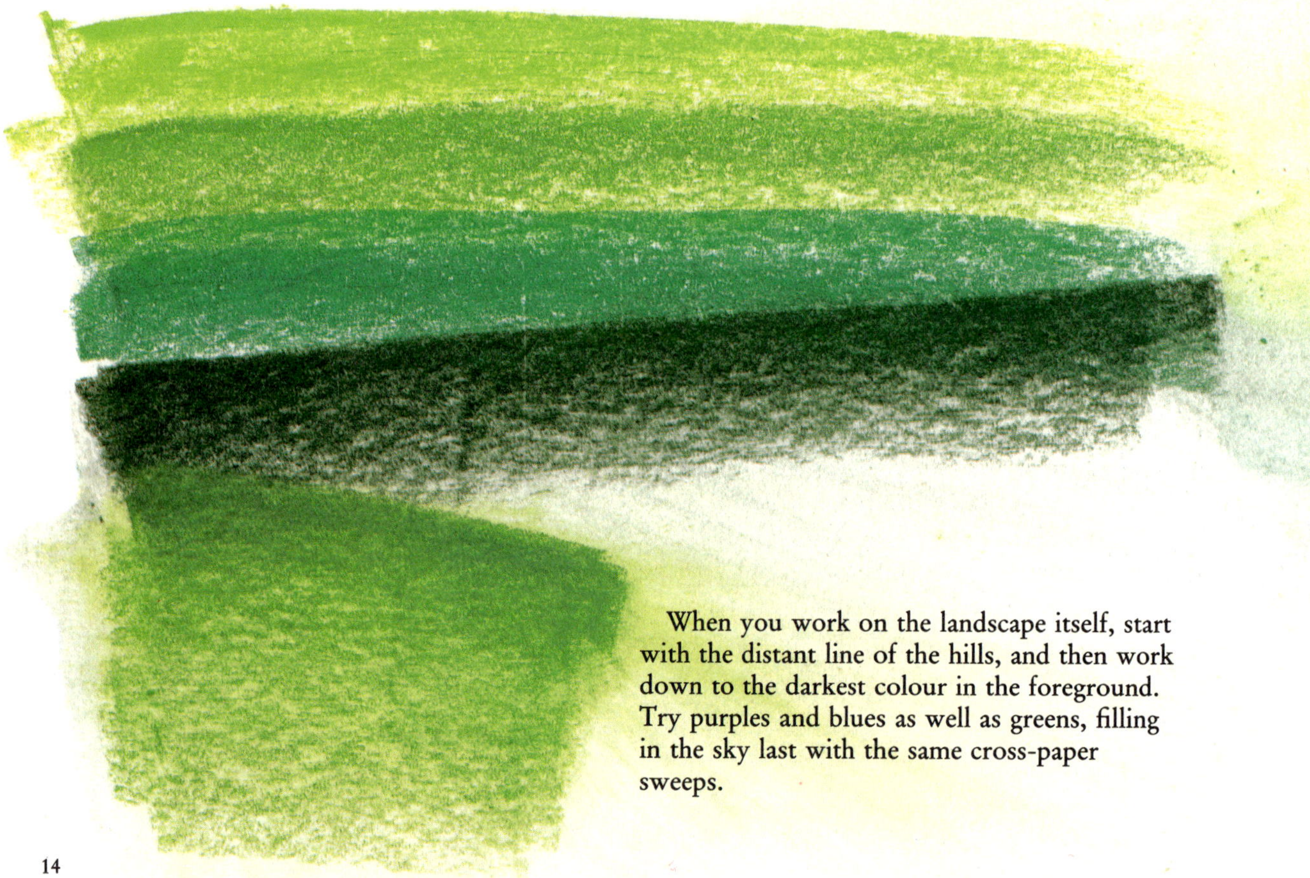

When you work on the landscape itself, start with the distant line of the hills, and then work down to the darkest colour in the foreground. Try purples and blues as well as greens, filling in the sky last with the same cross-paper sweeps.

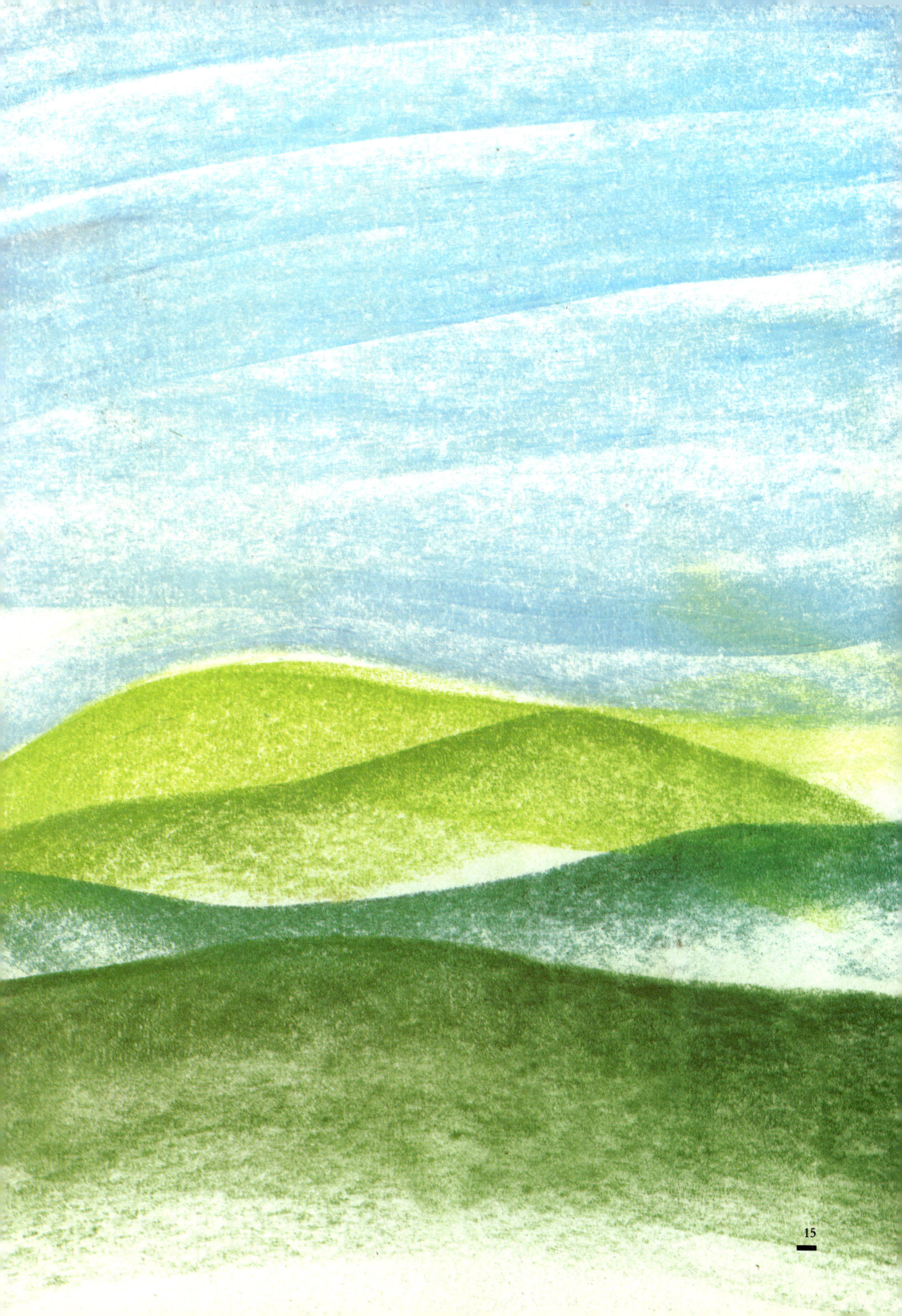

PART TWO: SIDE-STROKES

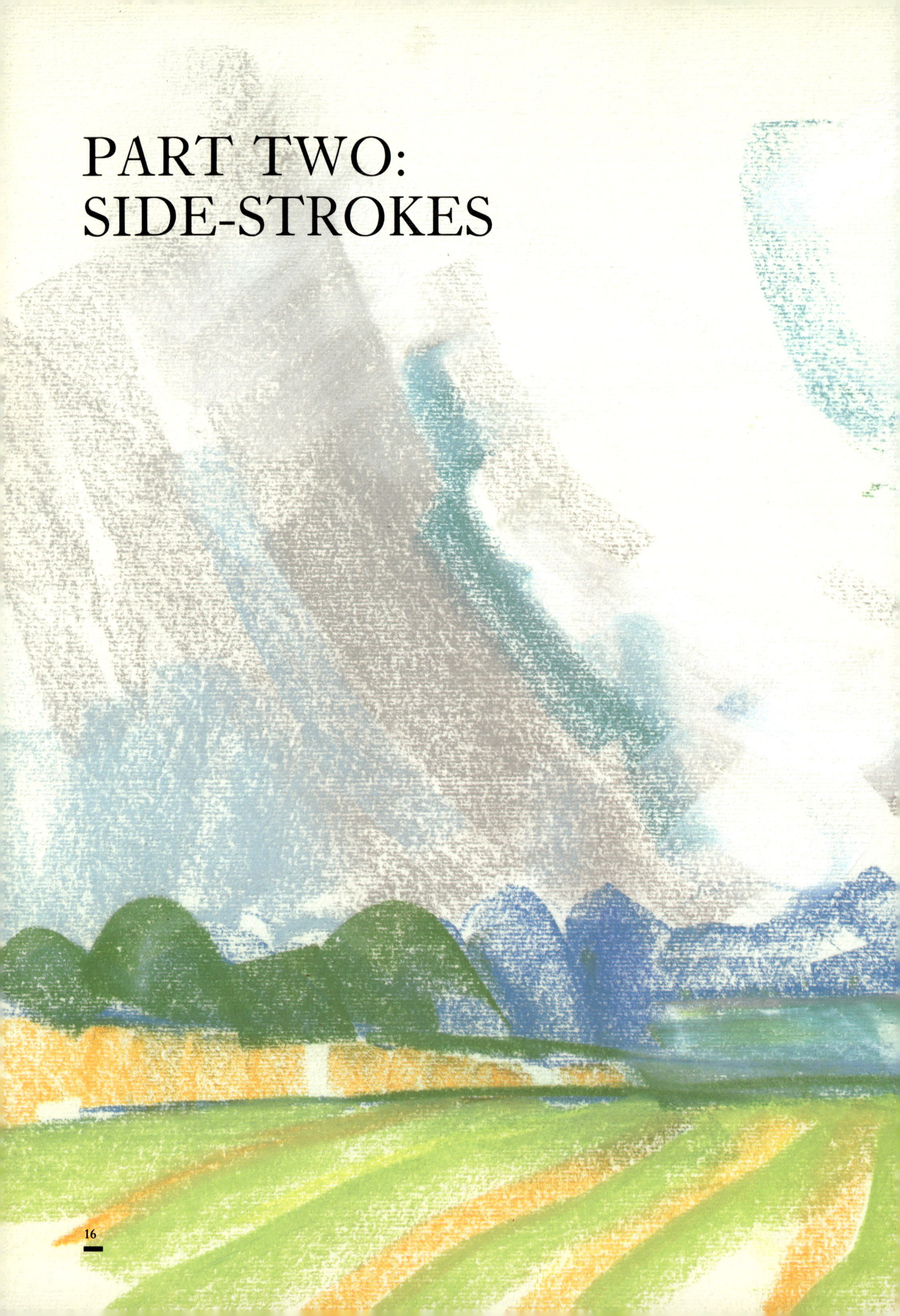

In Projects 1 and 3 we saw how important side-strokes are in the technique of using traditional soft pastels.

One advantage of learning how to manipulate lengths, rather than corners, of the sticks is that you can make parallel swathes of colour without any problem. You can quickly cover a lot of paper with crisp shapes, as you will see in the leeks of Project 4, or with colour upon colour, as in the cottages of Project 6.

Then there is pattern-making; with chalks of all kinds, side-strokes are irreplaceable for making consistent patterns over a substantial area. The brickwork in Project 1 was an introduction to this. A more controlled side-stroke is used to create the chequered tablecloth of Project 5, and the complicated and varied rhythms of the buildings in Project 6.

Pastel sticks do come in different sizes – some are distinctly thicker than others, and these last longer when used on their side. If you love the dash and verve you can achieve with side-strokes, then choose at least some of your colours from the heavier ranges.

Once you begin to break up sticks into various lengths, you may find that you end up with lots of small pieces. Make sure you have a sturdy protective box or container where even tiny lengths can be stored in safety.

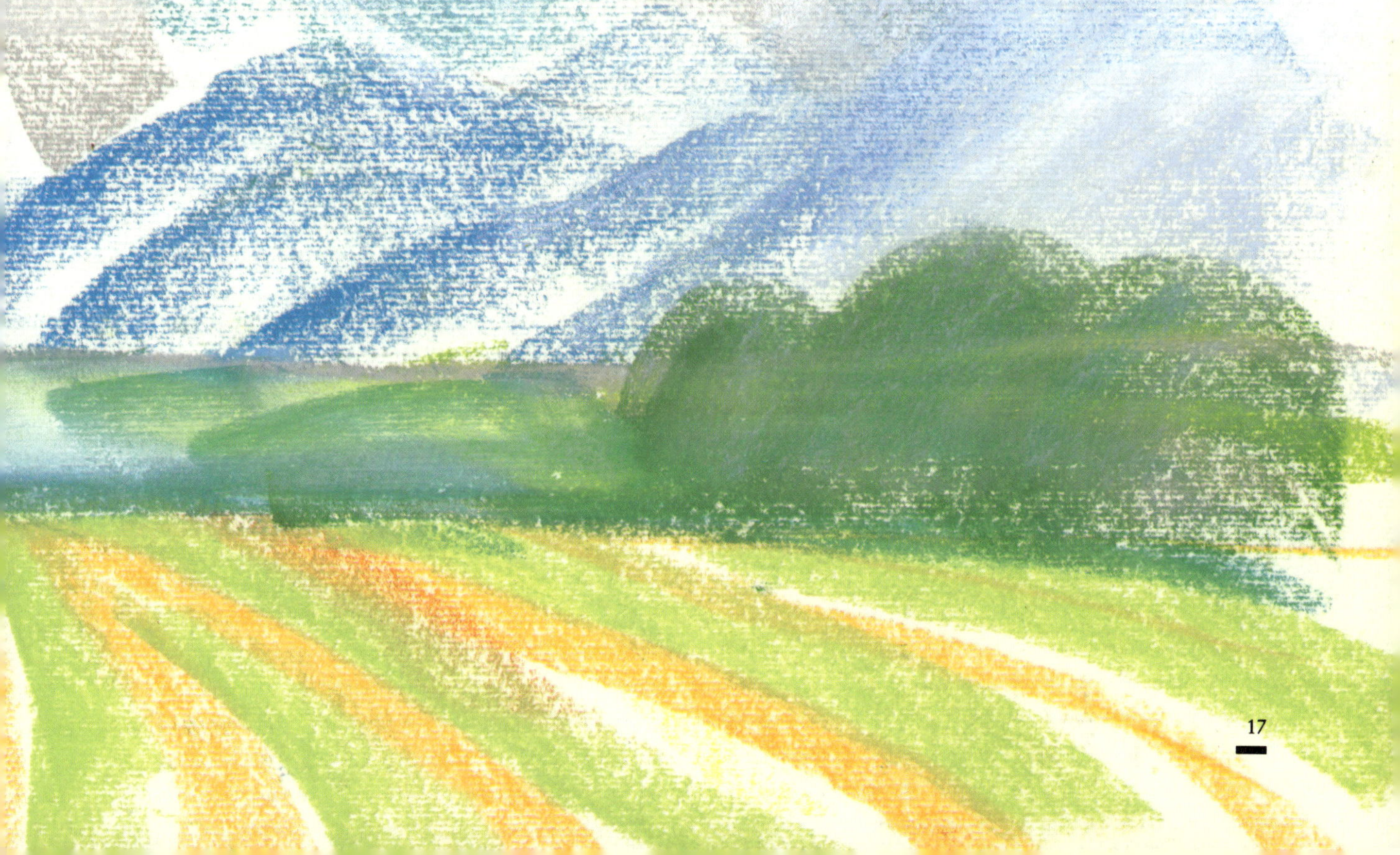

Leeks

For the landscape in Project 3, you began to use the long sweeps that make such effective shapes. Now you can be a little more precise. I've chosen leeks because their leaves make an ideal model: long, straight outlines, with only rounded edges and roots to be added.

When you break your pastel sticks, try to imagine how wide you want the side-strokes to be. You can easily mark the stick with a pencil if you don't trust your eye. Hold your fingers either side of the mark and break. You can cut sticks, too, but this seldom works for me; it often gives a much more crumbly and ragged edge.

With a fairly small piece of green, practise drawing longish strokes, changing the pressure from side to side to give a crisp edge. Try to start cleanly; put the stick down flat on the paper before you draw it across.

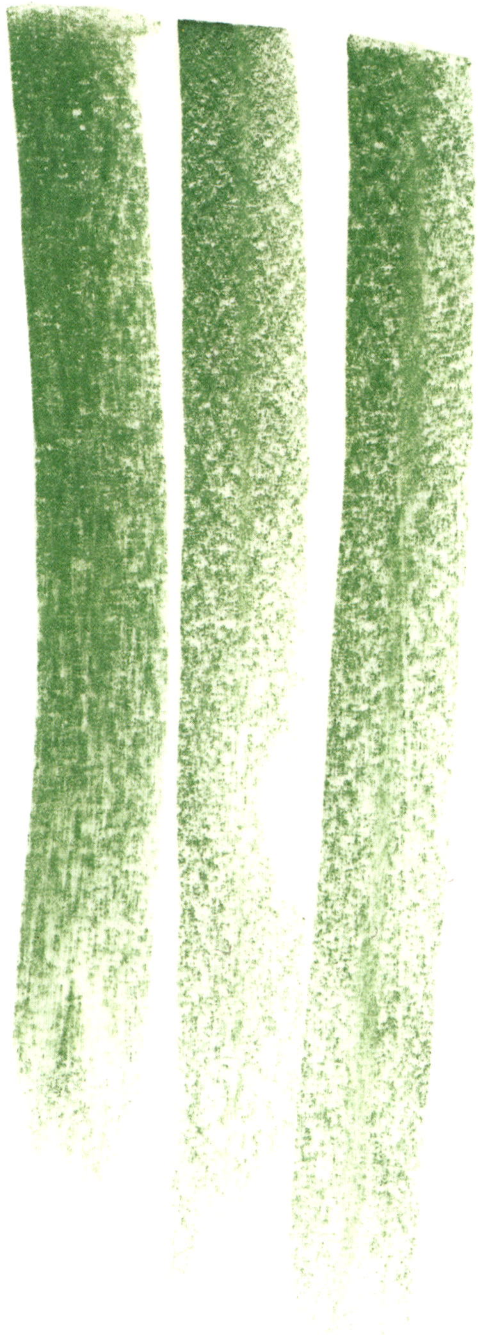

Now try lifting the pastel completely from one edge as you reach the edge of the paper. Look at the opposite page; you'll see that the suggestion of green along one side is quite enough to define the whole shape. It also means letting the paper work for you – leeks have a white base.

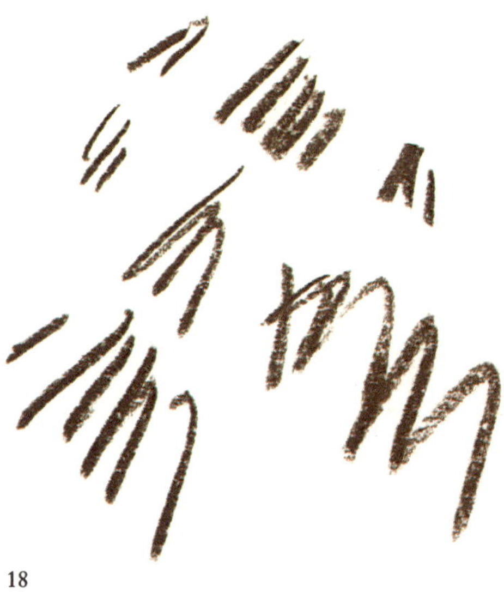

When you begin the project itself, keep the number of leaves on each leek to three, or the study will become complicated. The tops can be fairly uneven – few gardeners have leeks that grow in a straight line. Add a few brown roots, a line to mark the base, and the leeks are ready to go into the soup!

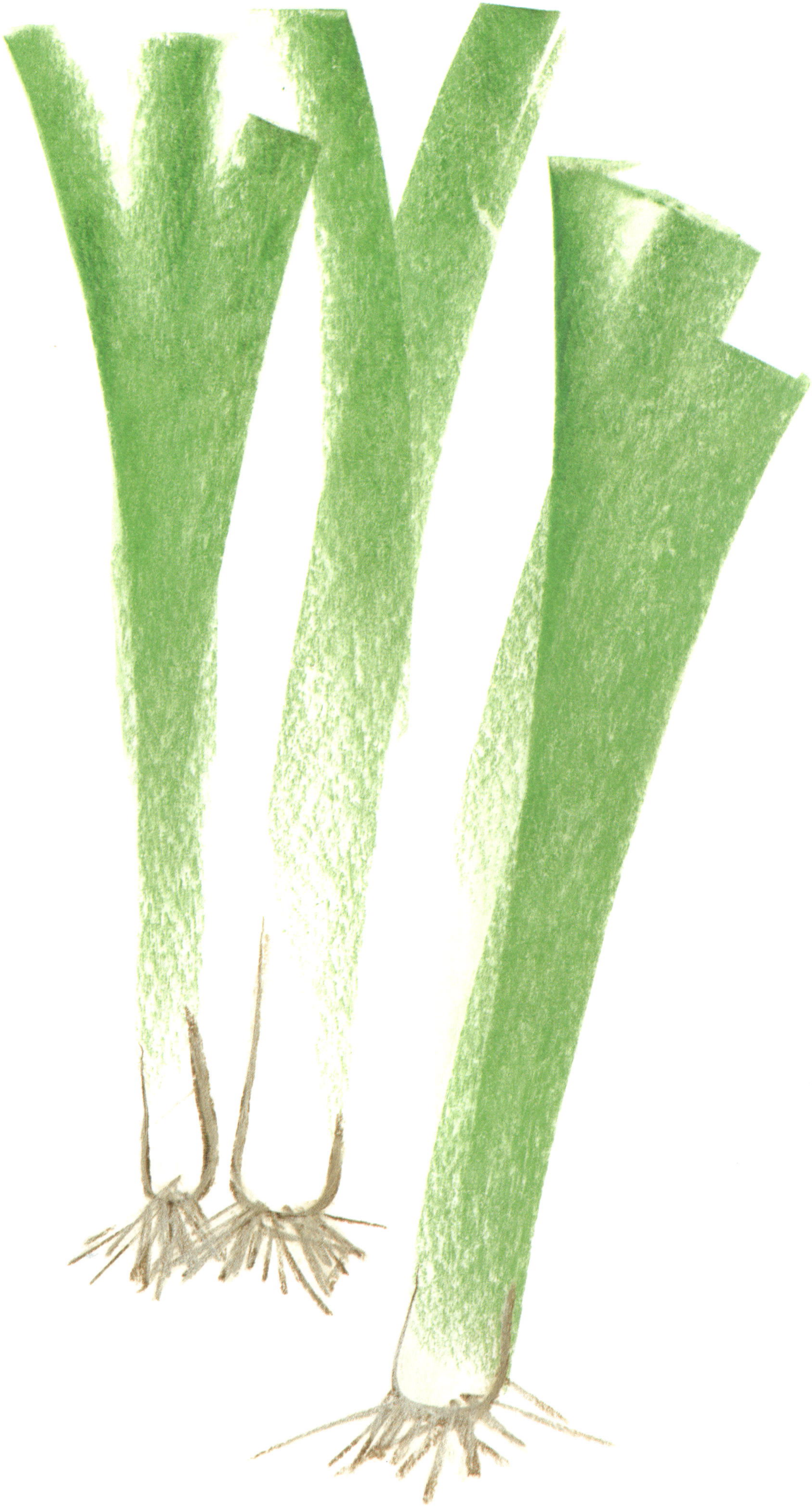

Chequered Cloth

Here is a sophisticated way of making side-strokes add depth and dimension to the simplest of studies. Renaissance painters knew all about squares used to create mathematical perspective, and the decreasing squares of a tiled floor in Dutch interiors added both atmosphere and an illusion of space to their paintings. But this chequered tablecloth is created much more easily, just by changing the direction of the squares from running across the cloth to down the side.

Start by practising with small sections of squares. If you need a little guidance, then lightly sketch in the line where the tablecloth falls over the edge of the table.

To make the pattern even, without effort, use the same piece of pastel all the way through. So begin with a new piece whose long edges are still sharp. See how much pressure you need to give you crispness, without pushing down so hard that the pastel crumbles. Every time you begin a new square, work in the same direction.

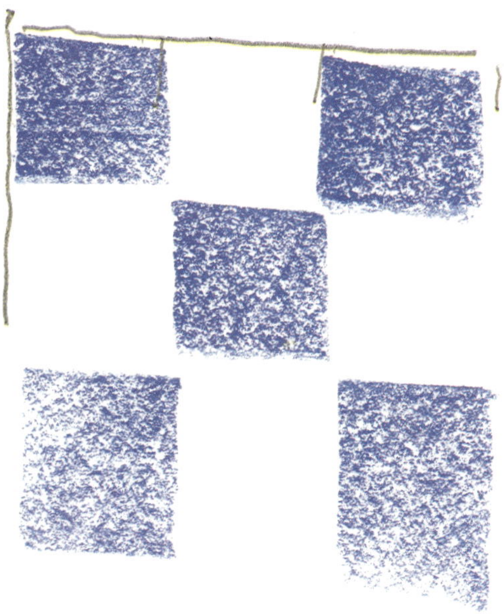

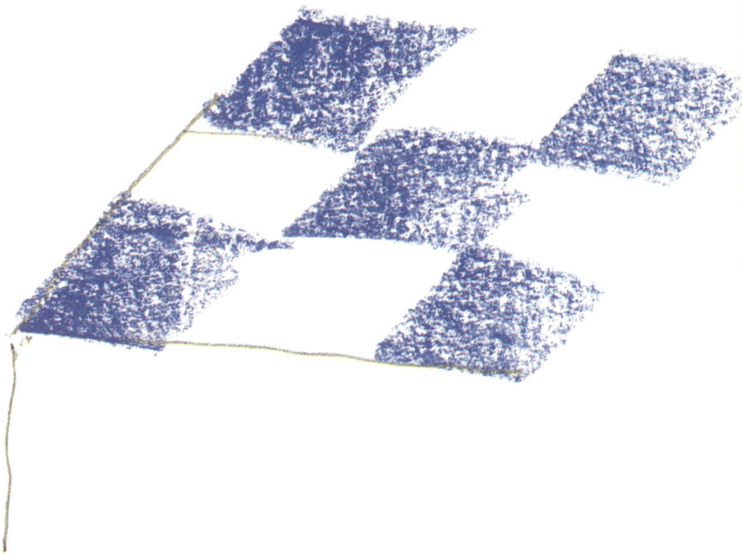

You can see that I worked from the dividing line down, and with the greatest pressure at the top right-hand corner. Then I worked from the dividing line up, shifting the stroke sideways to create an angle.

The bowl of flowers helps to give substance to the picture. You could also use an ornament, or a bowl of fruit. The background is as solid as possible to contrast with the pattern, and to let the illusion do its work.

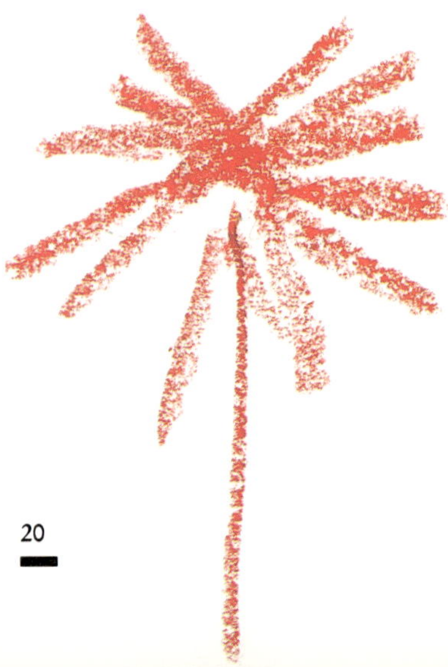

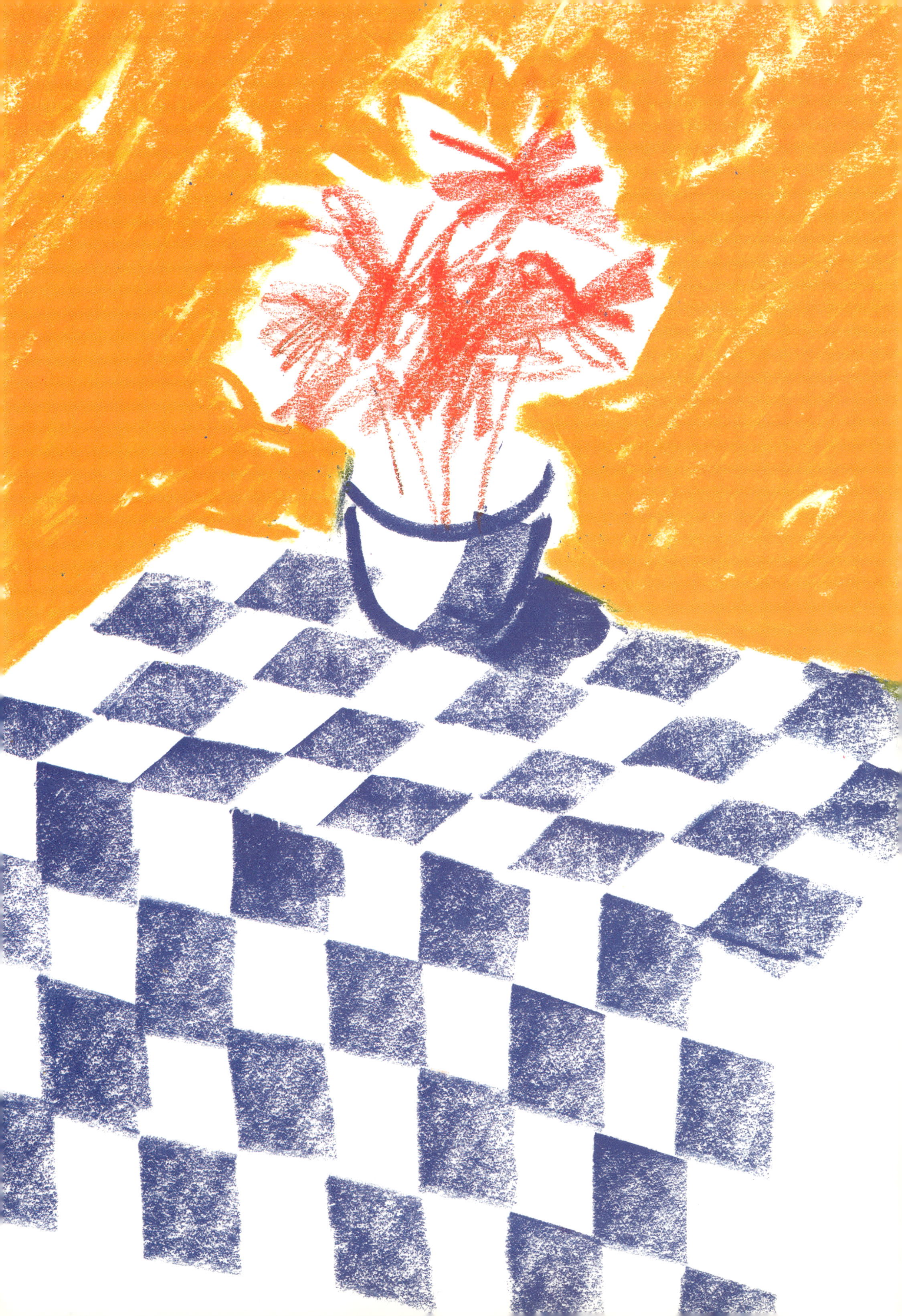

Cottages

In this study the side-strokes create a complicated mesh of colour and shapes. I chose a coloured paper to let the white window frames stand out.

The use of smaller pieces of pastel can be quite difficult, because they are sometimes hard to handle, but the square tops of the sticks are just not big enough to work with. However, choosing a subject like this, with many variations in colour and shape, means that you don't have to concentrate so much on precise edges to your strokes.

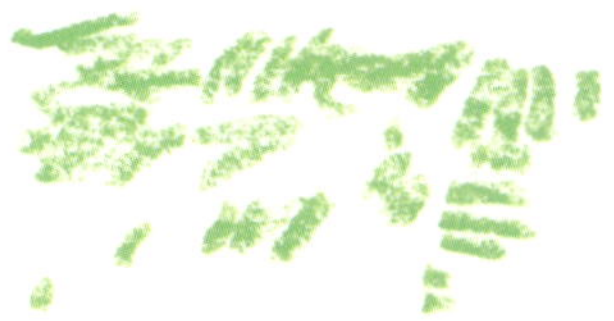

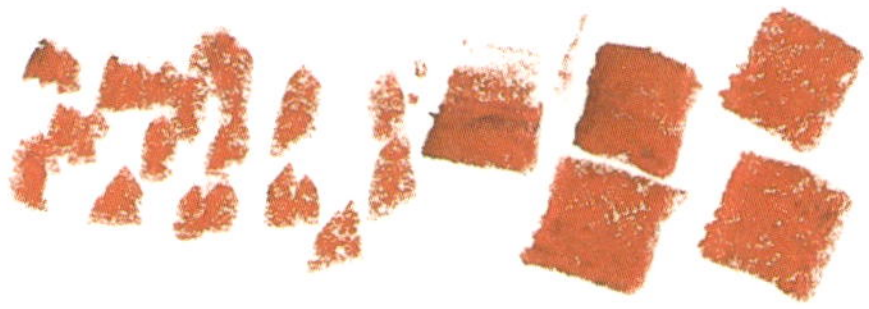

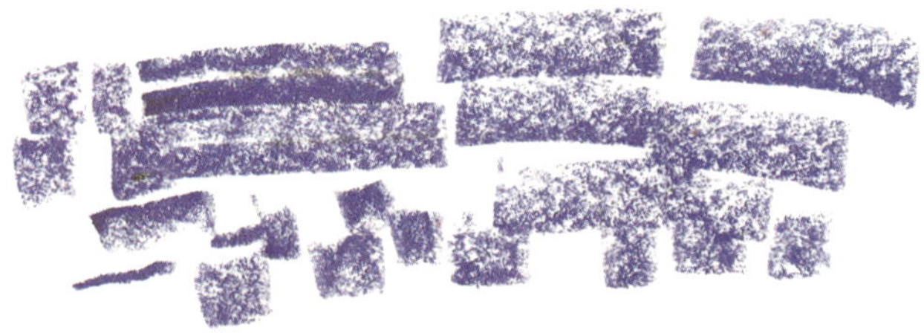

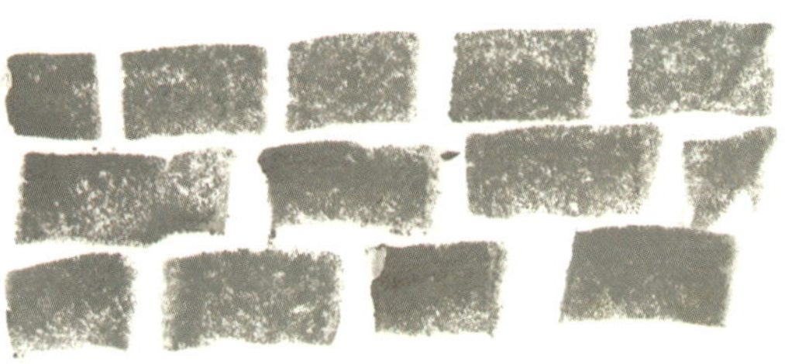

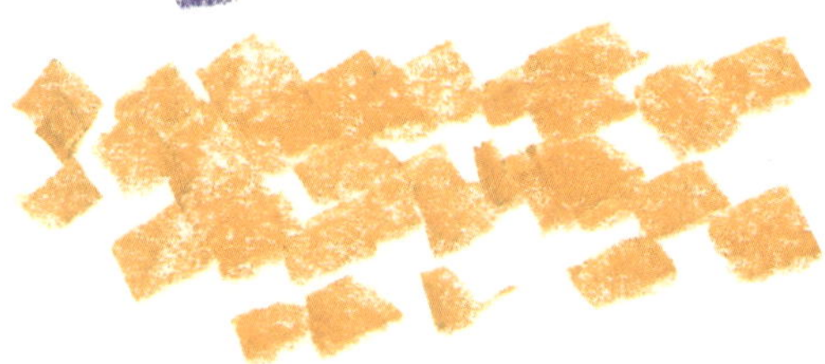

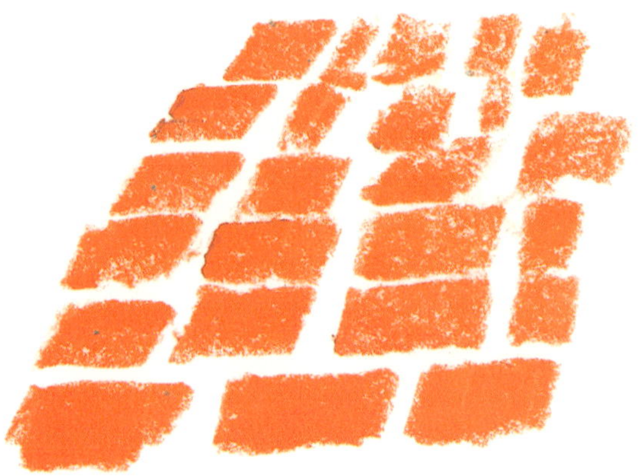

Practise manipulating the small pieces in different directions and in different patterns. When the spaces between the strokes are vertical, you will seem to be looking straight at the subject. When the spaces are left slanting in one direction, then the object will appear to slant away from you.

I began by drawing in the white window frames, and then filling in the walls and roofs. There is a slight change in the pattern of the two cottages that helps to differentiate them. The sky is added last of all, after the red chimneypots. You can blend the pastels with your finger to give a smooth appearance when necessary, as a contrast to the pattern in the rest of the picture. We'll be looking at blending more carefully in Part Five.

Be meticulous about blowing off any excess dust – each errant speck will stand out against the dark background like a spotlight!

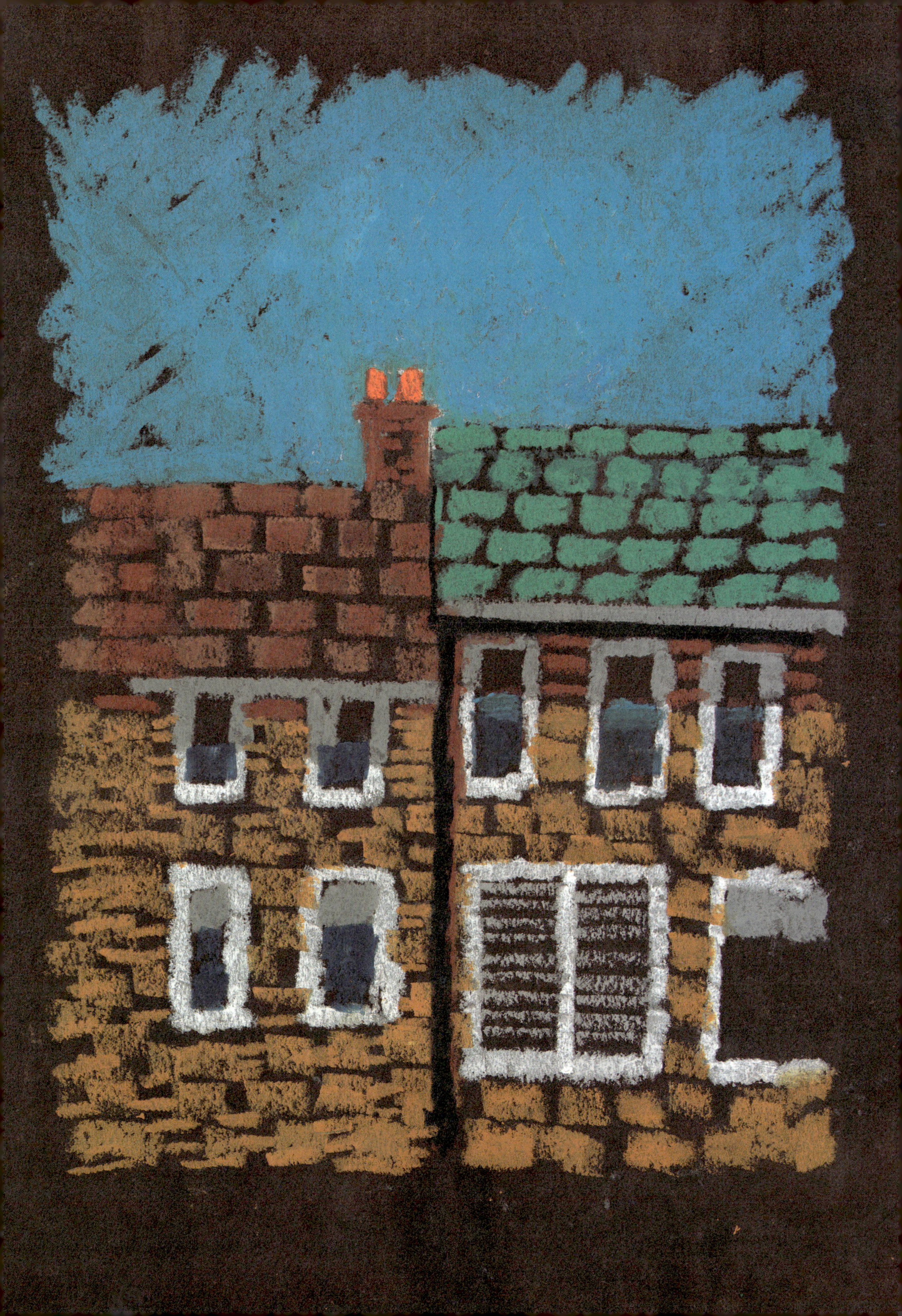

PART THREE: OIL PASTELS

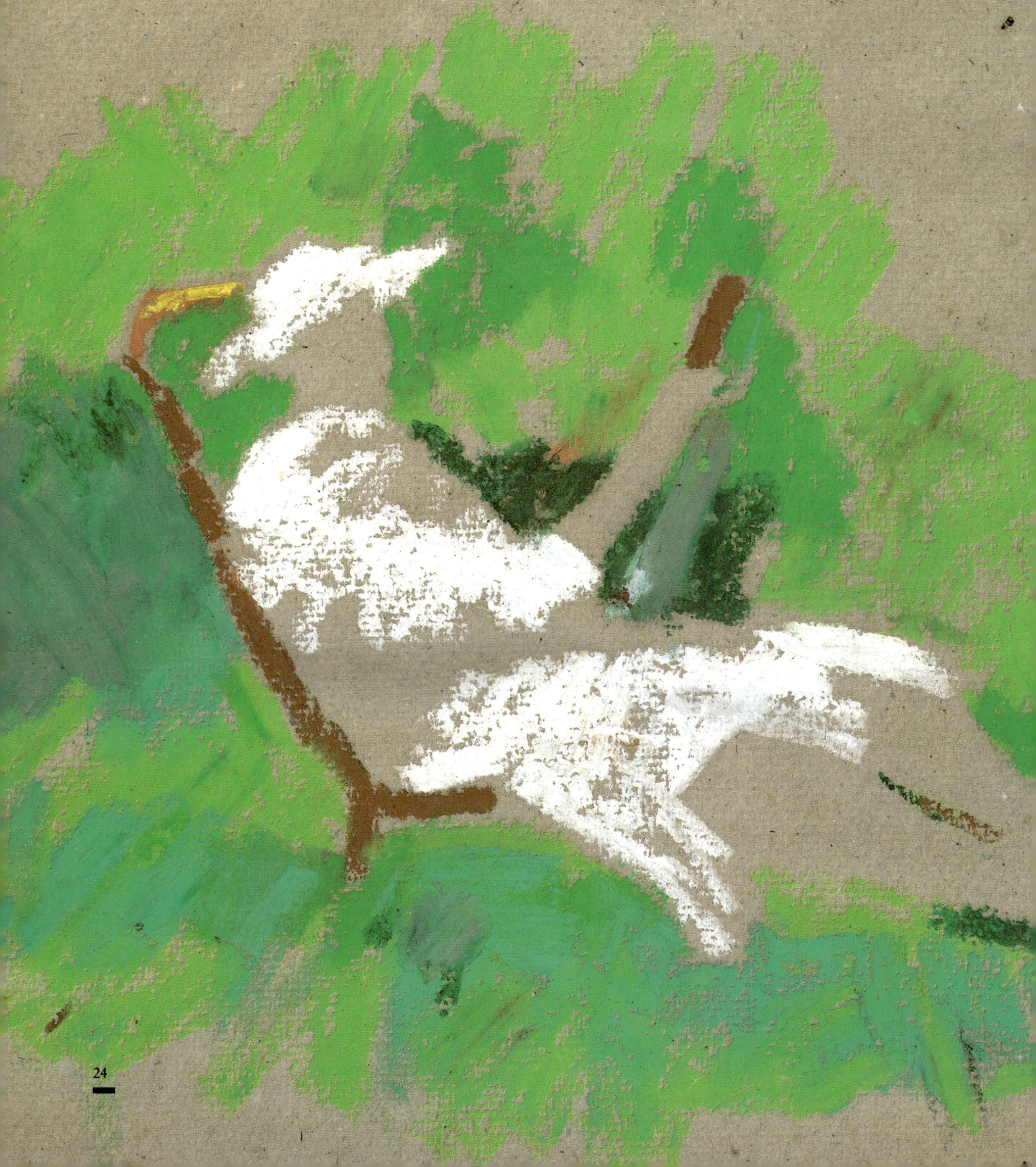

Although oil pastels are relatively new as a medium, experimental formulae and a few inventive artists have made a considerable impact on the market.

Oil pastels have a distinct quality of their own, and they are neither a substitute, nor a rival, for the soft sticks. There is a relatively modest range of colours, and they have certainly sacrificed subtlety of tone, but in return they give an incredible depth of colour and a brilliant surface, which no other drawing medium can match.

Any artist using pastels should experiment with the oil version. Like all mediums they have limitations, and I have to admit that I find it difficult to get a fine line or a flawless edge with them; however, you can choose your projects and your subjects to suit, concentrating on rich colours and broad shapes.

When you work on a final drawing, the edges of your work will tend to fade away rather roughly as the sticks lift off the paper. You can solve this problem by working the background right up to the edges of the paper, or at least just beyond the point where you can cover it with a mount.

Oil pastels are difficult to blend, and it takes quite a lot of pressure.

If you leave the box near a radiator or in sunlight, they get very dirty and sticky indeed, and you may find yourself with a pool of colour stuck firmly to the box. And what a waste of a wonderful medium that would be! So keep them covered, and in a cool place.

Box of Apples

If you look back to Project 2, the pavilion, you will see that I used blocks of colour with little depth or shadow. The shapes and shadows were modelled using separate colours, and you will see this technique used again with traditional pastels in Project 18. Here we need to look at substance in another way, so that the apples are moulded in tone as well as colour.

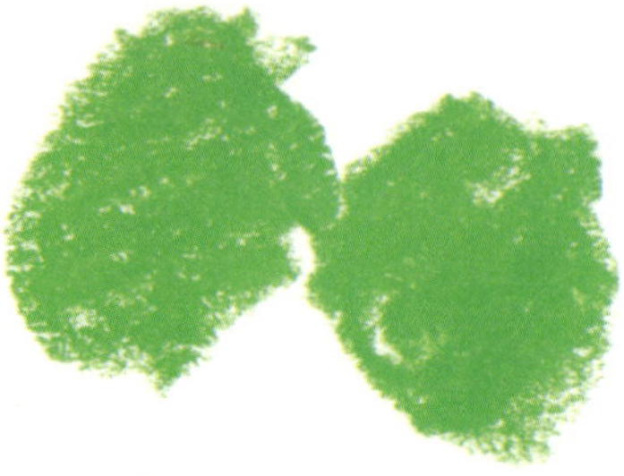

Start by drawing simple shapes, like green balls. Make a few round strokes in slightly darker green, then use an even darker green right at the base where the ball disappears against the background.

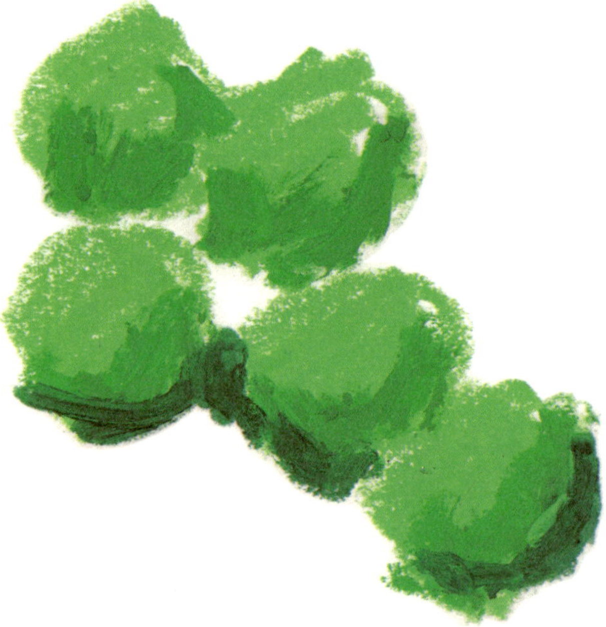

The highlight is usually a point of white. When light hits an object it creates a sparkle or shine that deflects the eye from the colour beneath. If you were working on a tinted paper, you would use white oil pastel, but working on white paper, I have simply left a small space clear. Highlights are always on the side away from the shadow.

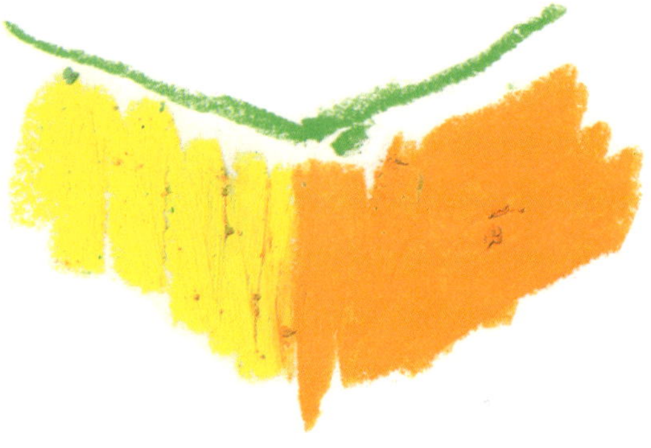

The box follows the same tonal method. The side nearest you is in shadow, so it becomes darker than its yellow body. I have left lots of white space to add sparkle. Oil pastels are quite heavy in texture, and I think they need a good bit of white to lift the effect.

When you work on the finished sketch, you can emphasize the apples by using a background. You often see fruit embedded in blue paper, and I think that particular colour makes the perfect complement to the fruit.

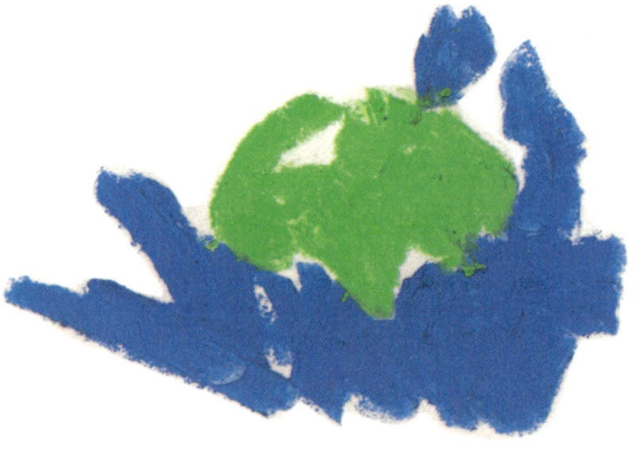

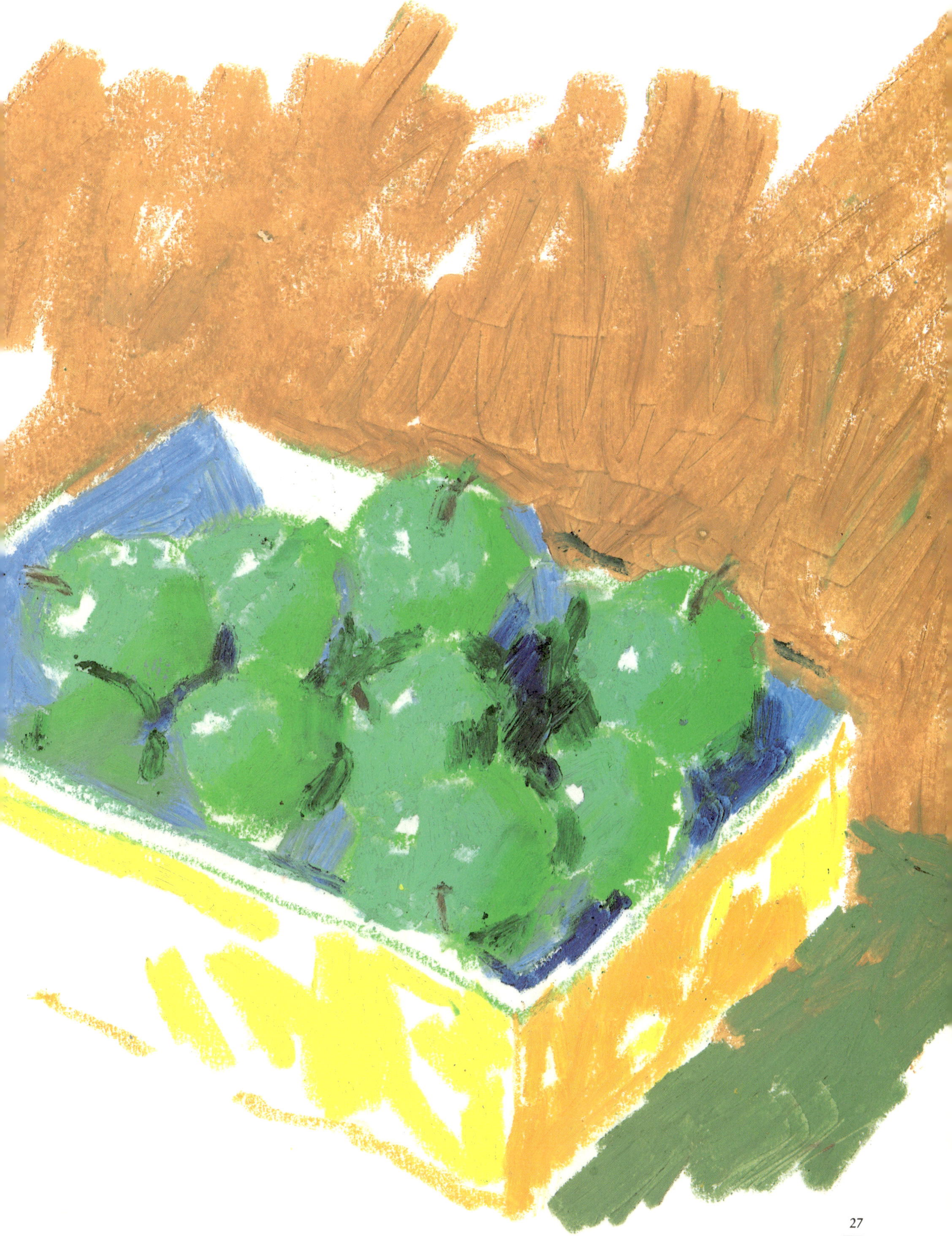

Georgian Square

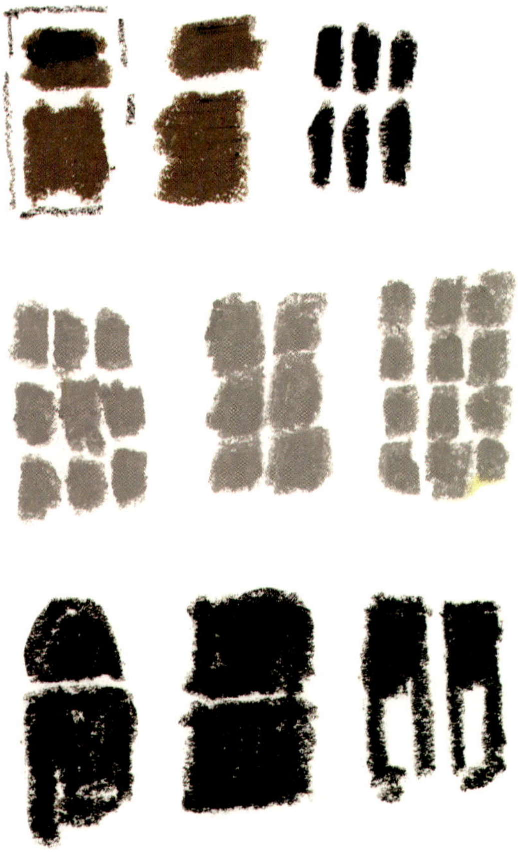

In Project 3 the receding colours of the pastel strokes gave an impression of disappearing hills. Oil pastels are not as subtle in their colours as the soft sticks, and it makes a progression of tones more difficult to achieve. So when I work with this medium in landscape I look for other ways of establishing space.

This view across a London square gave me the perfect focal point – an old tree stood in the square, between my seat and the house. It became a strong feature, not particularly because of its size or spread (compared to the house it had neither) but because of its position. With its roots running down to the ground in front of the square's planted edge, it created a very definite space between itself and the house behind it.

Practise the short strokes that make up the windows, leaving the actual frames white. Note the idiosyncratic variation in the window mouldings: some frames are the original six-light sashes, others are Victorian replacements. Many old houses have similar mixtures.

The bulk of the house is left as plain white paper. When you begin the final sketch, make a very light charcoal drawing of the outline of its shape, the roof, and the divisions that create bays for the windows.

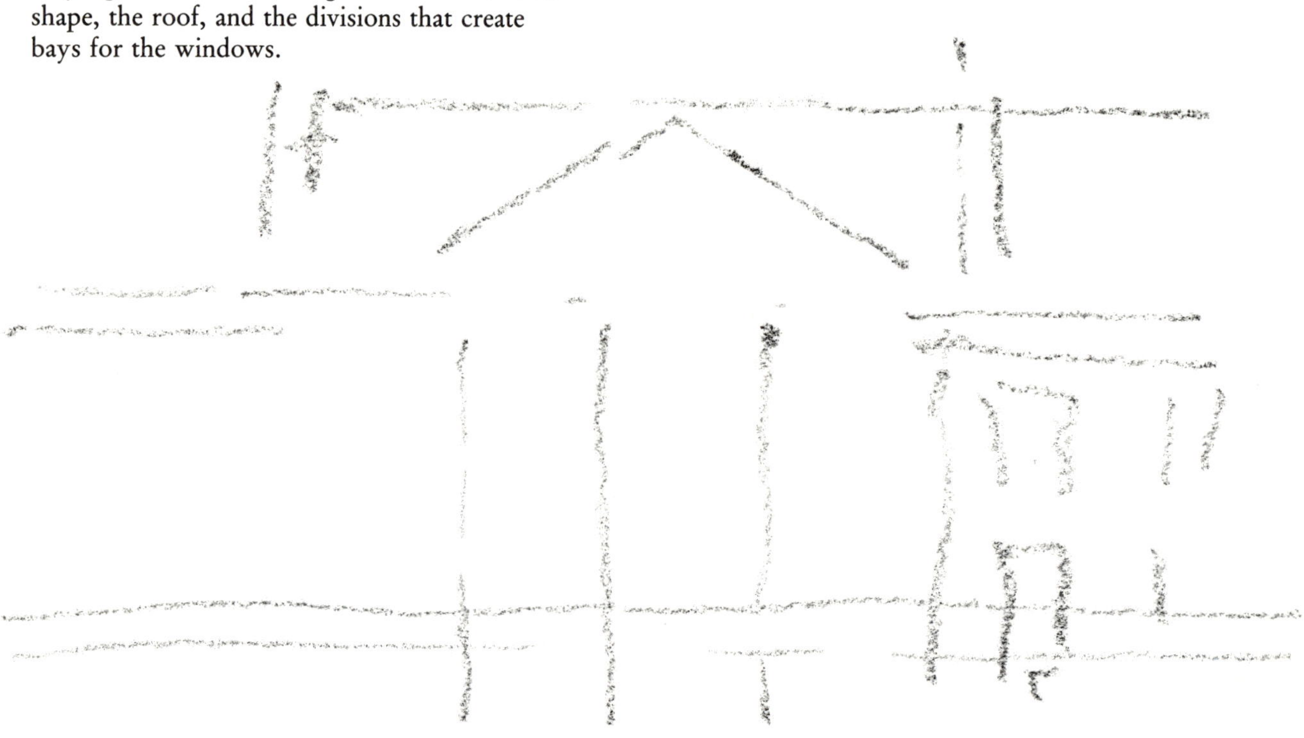

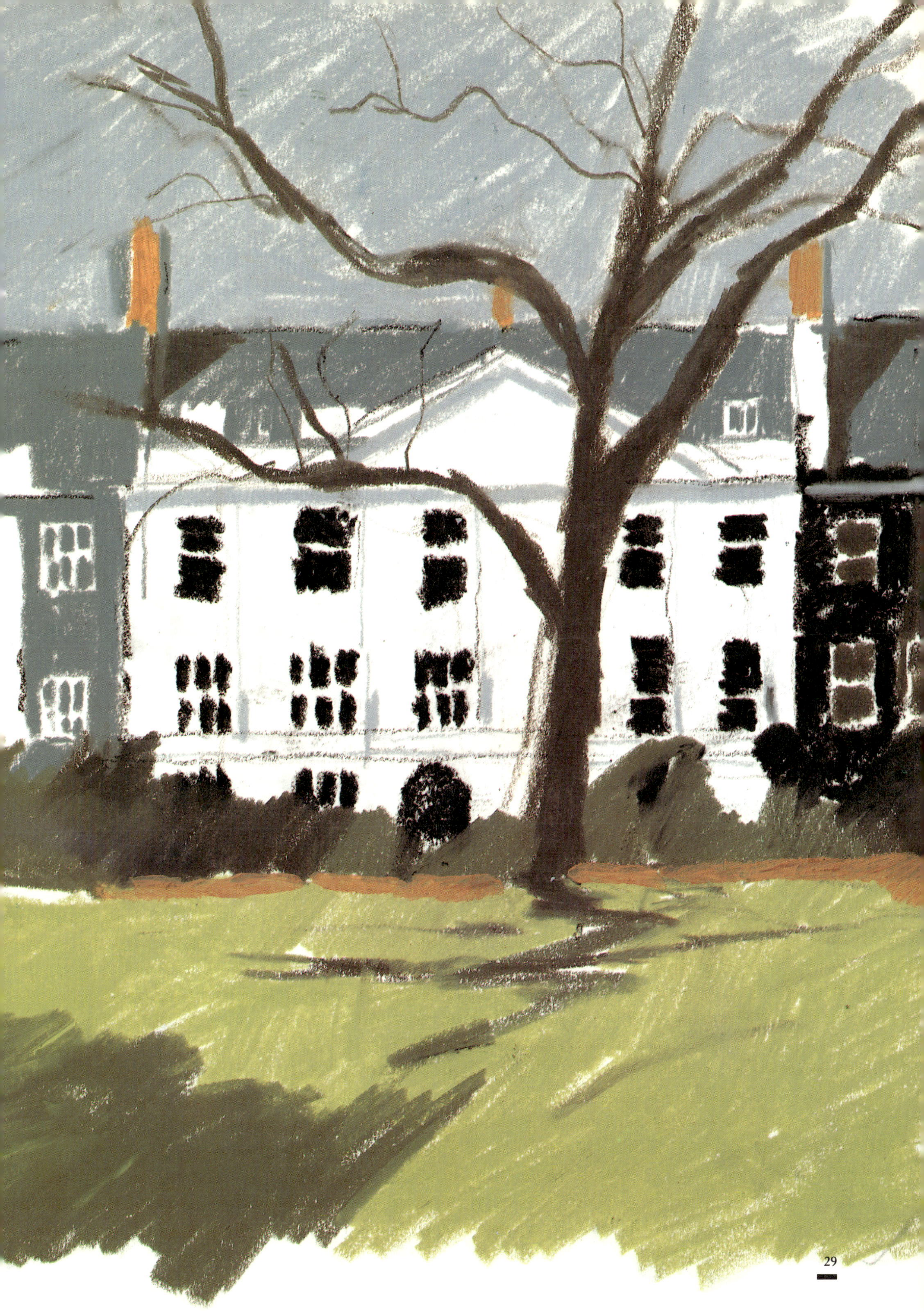

Project 9 Moving Shadows

River Pool

The lovely watery colours of blue and green are always attractive, and never more so than when used together in similar tones, intermingling like the images in a reflecting pool. Oil pastels are the perfect medium, as their glimmering surface works well with the sunlit sparkles on the water. Soft sticks would be lifeless and dull by comparison. The choice of medium can be as important as the choice of subject.

Start by making the fish shapes; work out variations with larger tails, longer fins, and see which you prefer. The light reflects off the silvery scales around their heads, so I left those white.

We usually imagine that water is blue or grey. However, river water is brown or green, because of reflected plants, algae, etc. Shadows can be dark green, blue or even grey. I chose to use a bright blue shadow simply to make the other colours even more luscious. The yellow fish seemed to hang quietly in the water, their fins moving almost imperceptibly as they kept their positions.

Rippling, long wriggles give water the feeling of movement. Many wave patterns are horizontal, from a surface disturbance, but I chose the image of weed rising in vertical waves to emphasize depth. A rippling stem in front of one of the fish increases the impression of distance.

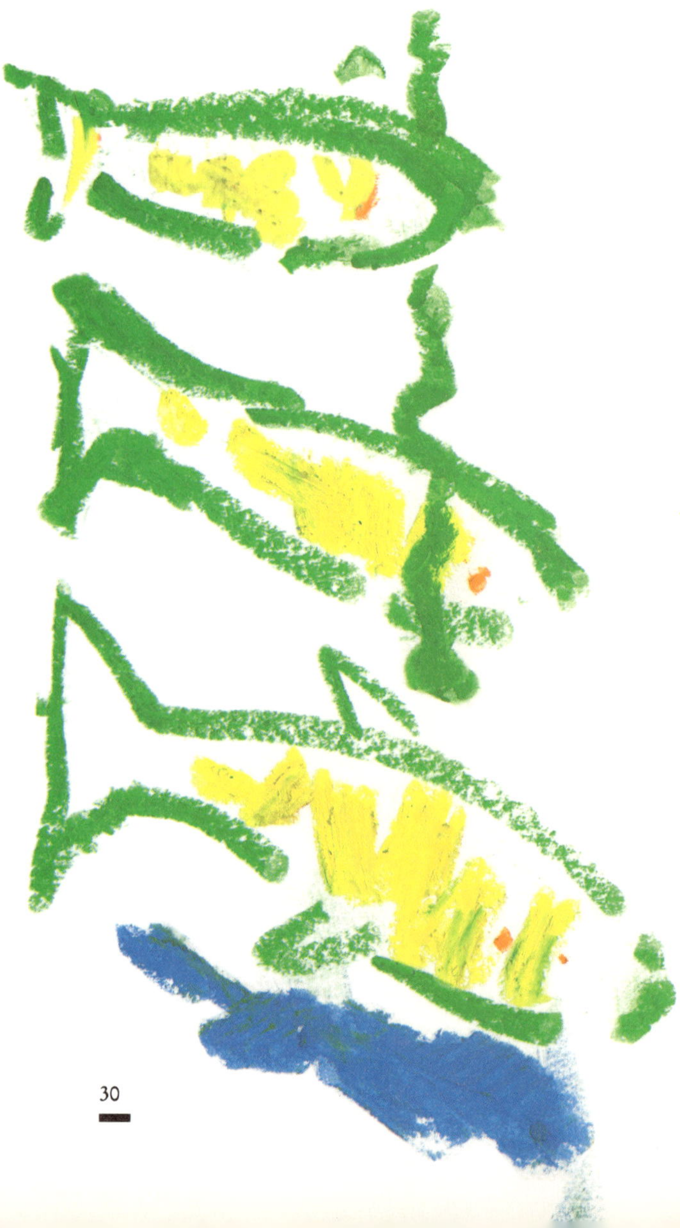

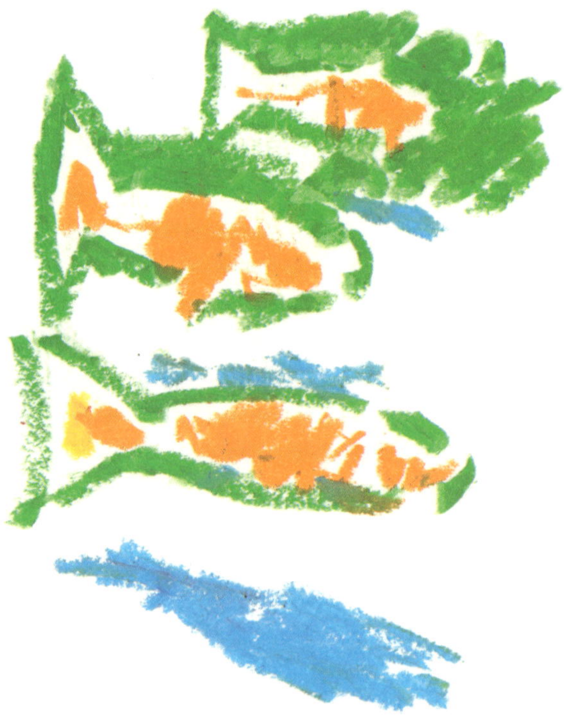

Each fish has its corresponding shadow on the river bed. The shadow will be increased or diminished by the angle of the light coming through the water. Here, with the light behind me, the shadows were thinner and appeared shorter than the fish above.

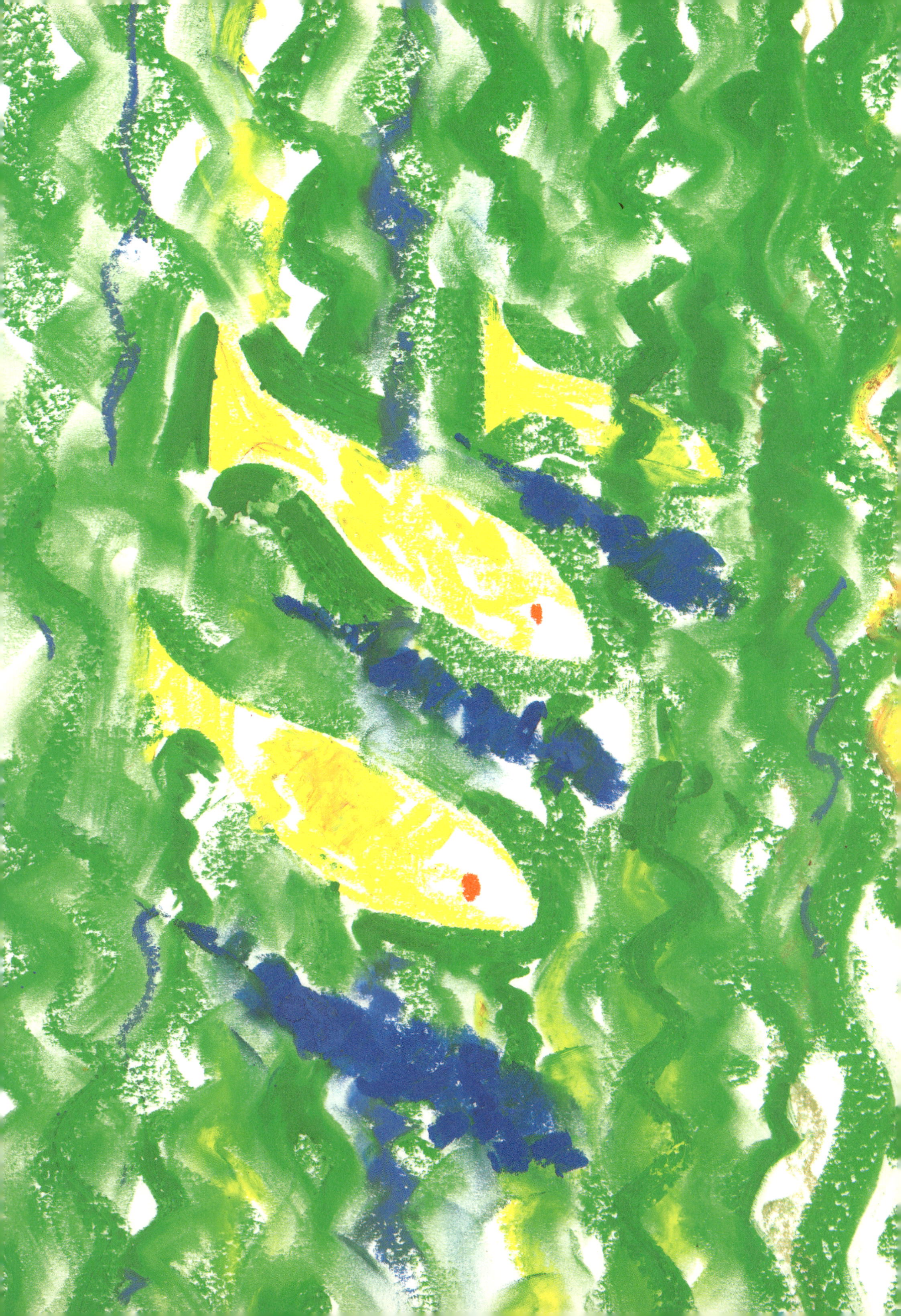

PART FOUR: MORE ABOUT DRAWING

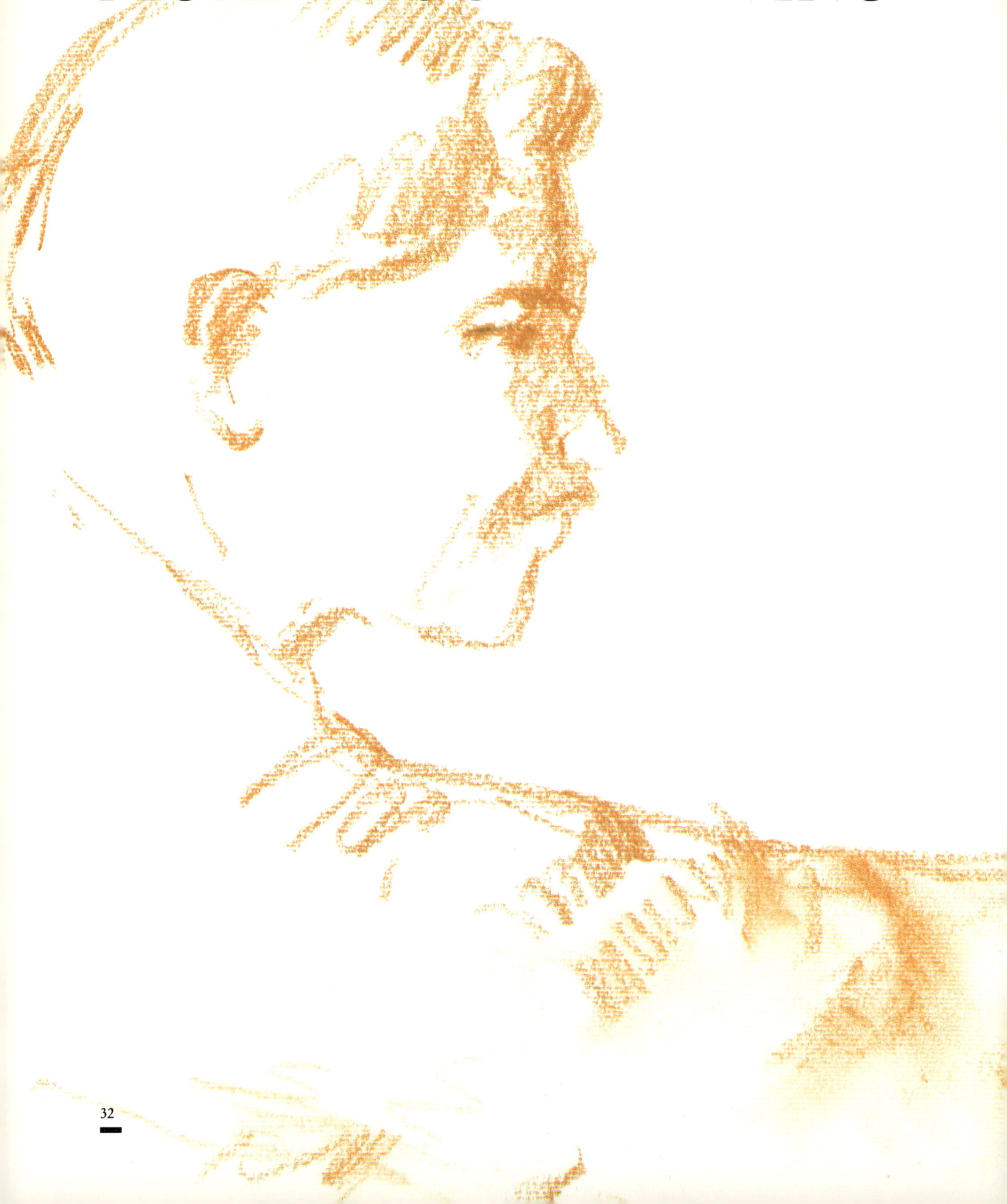

In a real sense, pastel is probably the oldest art medium of all, as historians believe that prehistoric cave drawings were painted with black, brown and red earth colours, made into chalks.

Renaissance painters used sienna, a reddish chalk that gave both colour and texture to their drawings. Multicoloured chalks were not developed until the eighteenth century, when artists such as Fragonard and Boucher made magnificent use of them for portraits, as well as for sketches for their other paintings.

By the end of the nineteenth century, Degas and Renoir were among the leading artists who adopted pastels almost as a signature, particularly for quick sketches made on the spot. They utilized the medium so well that many contemporary pastel artists have been too inhibited by their reputations to develop styles and techniques of their own.

Today all that is changing; soft sticks in myriad colours and even in different textures encourage modern artists, who appreciate the value of an infinitely variable medium with a unique textural quality.

Whatever your previous experience, learning to use these soft sticks will quickly give you an artistic vocabulary quite different from any other, and perhaps with less effort!

Hand Sketches

Black and brown earth colours can be harsh; the red sienna used by the old masters softened to warm, flesh shadows on their creamy paper. Today sienna is still a favourite of life-class students for the same reason.

Artists often use line and shadow to create a three-dimensional image, and when restricted to one colour, lighter and darker tones are used in place of lighter or darker colours.

Drawing your own hands is one of the first exercises for a new artist, and one of the everlasting preoccupations of experienced ones! Pastel makes it particularly easy, because you can smudge the outlines to create effective and pleasing shadows without changing sticks.

Assuming you are right-handed, put your left hand on the table in front of you, on top of the pad. (Reverse that if you use your left hand for drawing.) Bending your fingers will give the shape a little more definition.

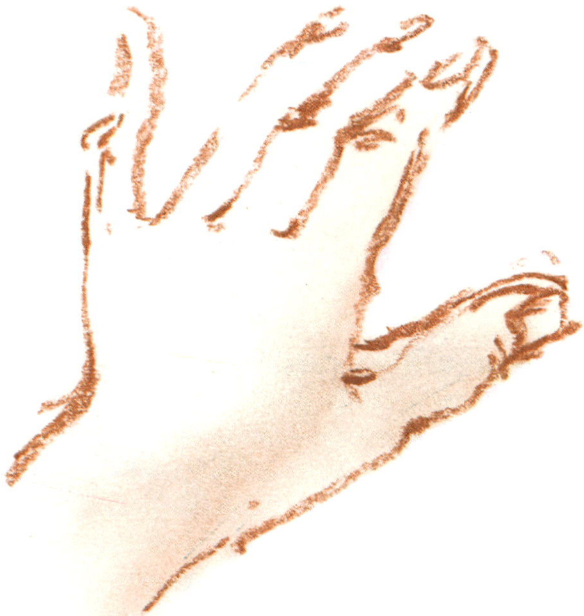

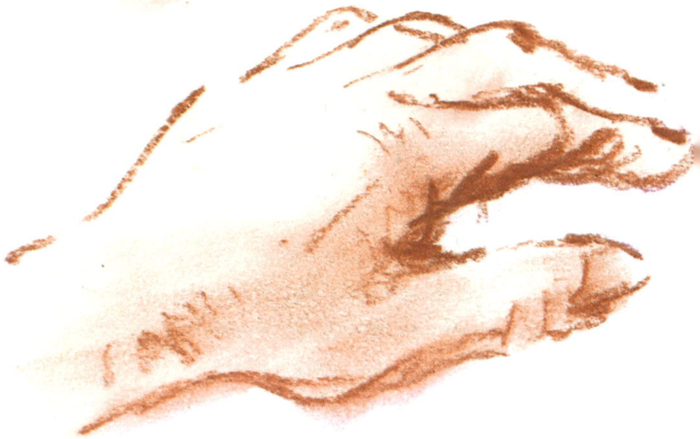

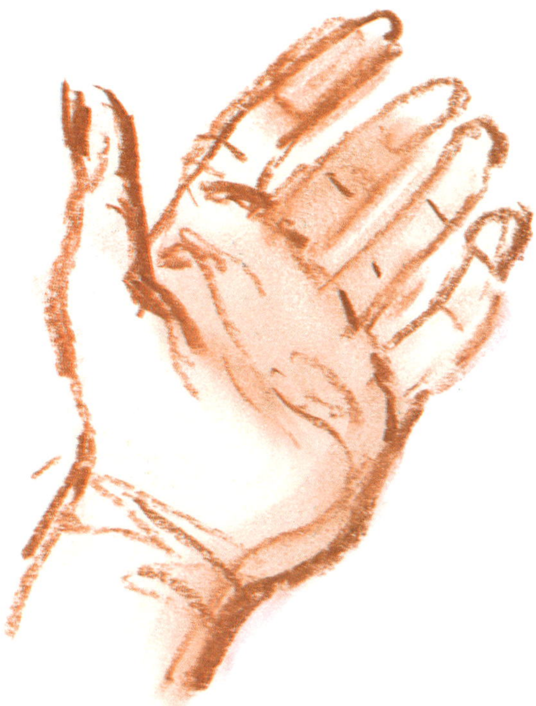

Work as fast as you can. Drawing like this should be quick and light; if you try to be too careful it will tighten your drawing hand, as well as your modelling hand on the other side.

Smudge the pastel in places where you want to create darker shadows, like the area underneath the rounded thumb. Sometimes you may need to add extra lines over the smudge to give a fillip to the wrinkles in fingers or wrist.

When you are ready to work, leave enough room on the paper to draw your hand at least twice – somehow multiple images look fresher than a single, hard-worked sketch.

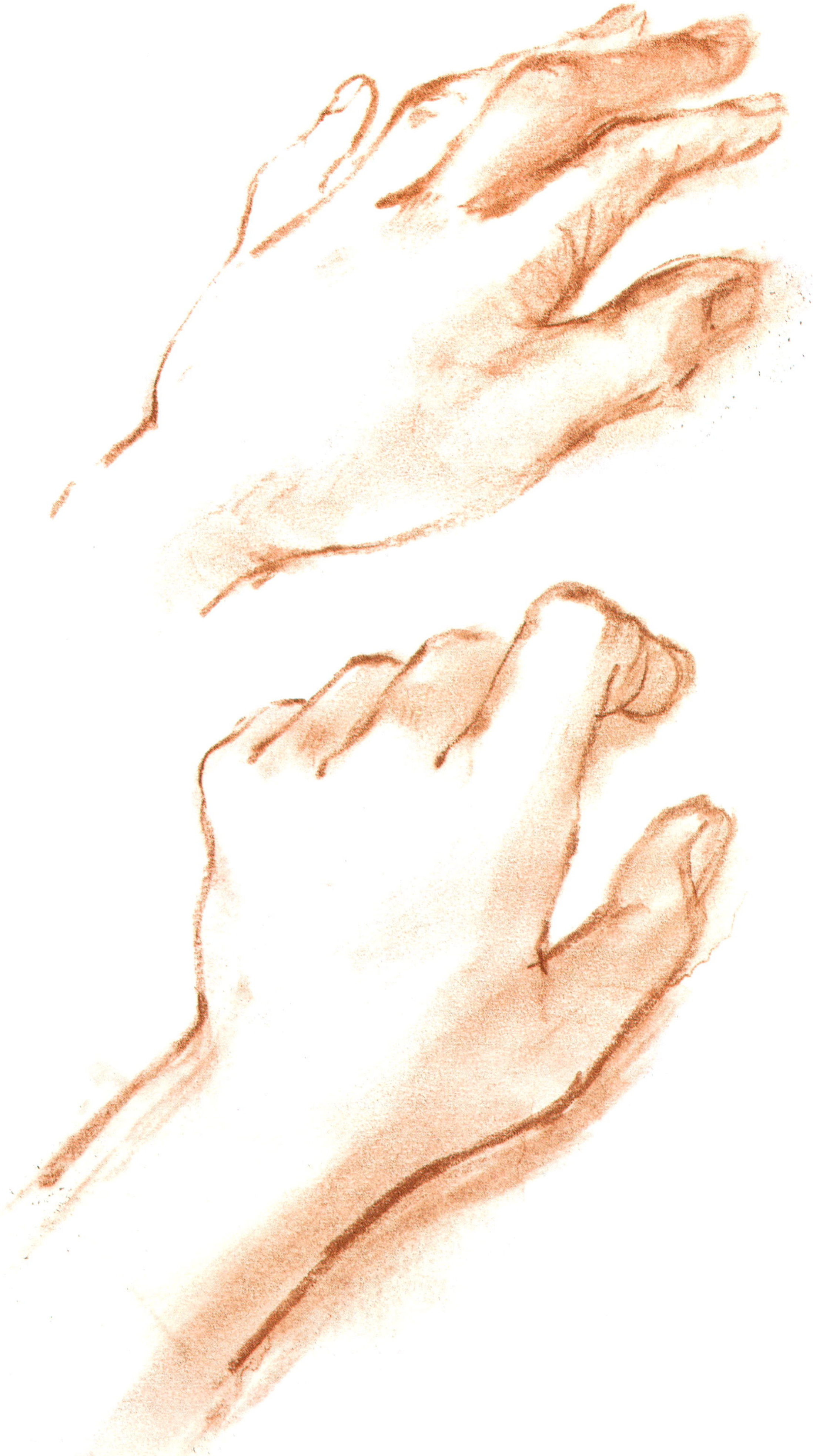

Grey Silk Hat

One of the affinities between medium and subject is apparent when you use pastel to draw fabric of any kind. Somehow the undulating surface of the tinted paper and the flecks of colour match the flow of satin and silk.

Try and find a similar hat to work from; the brim should be stiff enough to give some shape, but soft enough to droop a little. Tie an old scarf around the crown; it doesn't matter what colour, as long as it swishes off the brim.

Prop the hat on a stand, or use an old vase, which you should ignore when you start drawing. Practise making simple oval sweeps. See the hat in its broad geometric shape rather than its detail, and keep your wrist light and flexible – you want a very subtle line, not a heavy mark. Now do two circles on top of each other, one soft grey for definition, one white for sparkle. Remember to keep the pastel skimming over the paper.

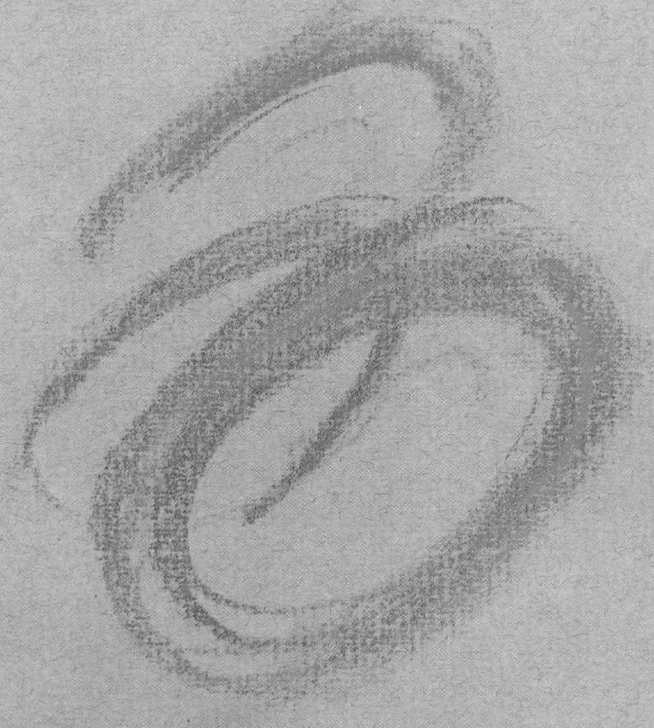

Look at the change from brim to crown. Try to pick up the slight bulging outline where the crown rises, and the folds of the scarf. Turn the hat in different directions until you are happy with the result.

Your fingers are the best tool for smudging. Try different fingers to get larger or smaller areas. Even your palm can be used, but always keep the pressure light. You will soon be able to judge how to get the effect you want.

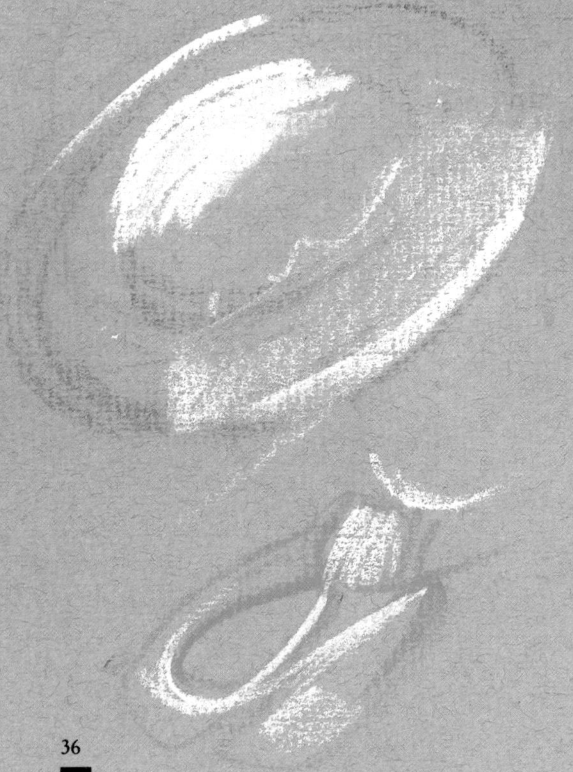

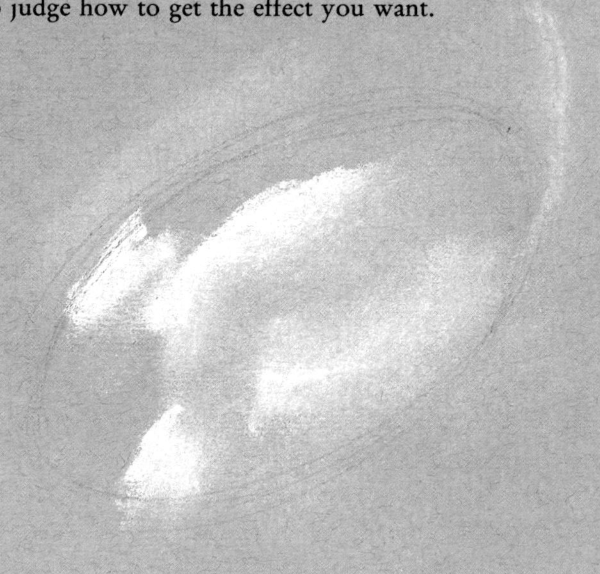

Add extra strokes of white where you see highlights. Finally a few soft lines, smudged, make a hatstand in the shadows.

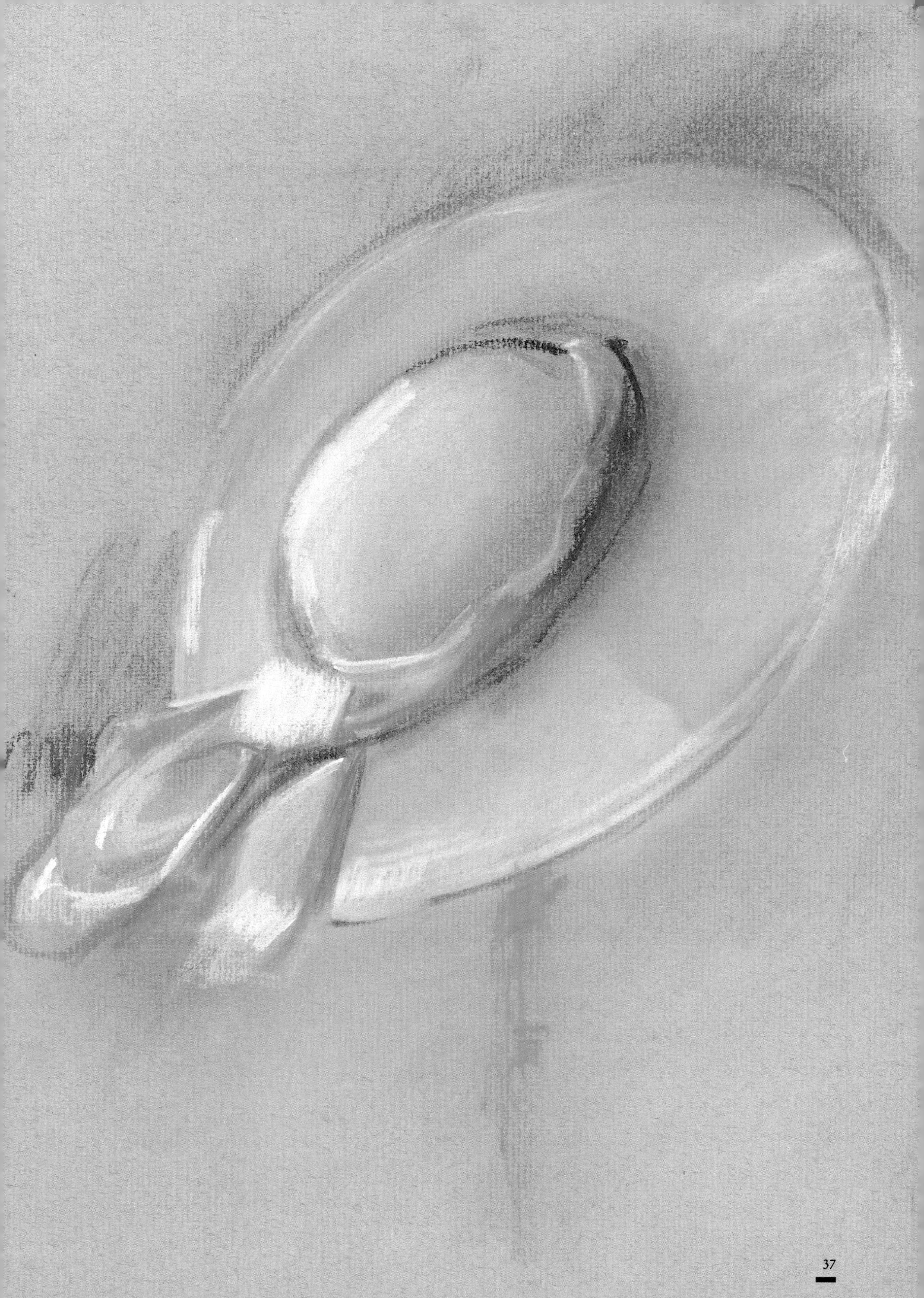

Project 12 Drawing on Rough Paper

Geraniums

Soft pastels are unmistakable in texture; they leave a 'snail trail' where the colour just catches the paper. When the paper is rough enough to have a texture of its own, you can achieve a particularly light effect, which seems to dance over the surface. Use the edge of the stick to skim as quickly as possible over the top. The combination here of generous leaves with comfortably irregular edges, rounded and much smaller circles for the flowers, and the two simple homely pots makes a fine composition.

Looking at the pots at a slight angle will add interest. I put mine on a low table to one side. Start by catching the rhythm of the leaves. They fold over and flop about in really delightful ways. Don't worry about repeating the exact pattern, just get a feel for geranium leaves with their crinkled edges. You can use the information stored in your head later in other drawings.

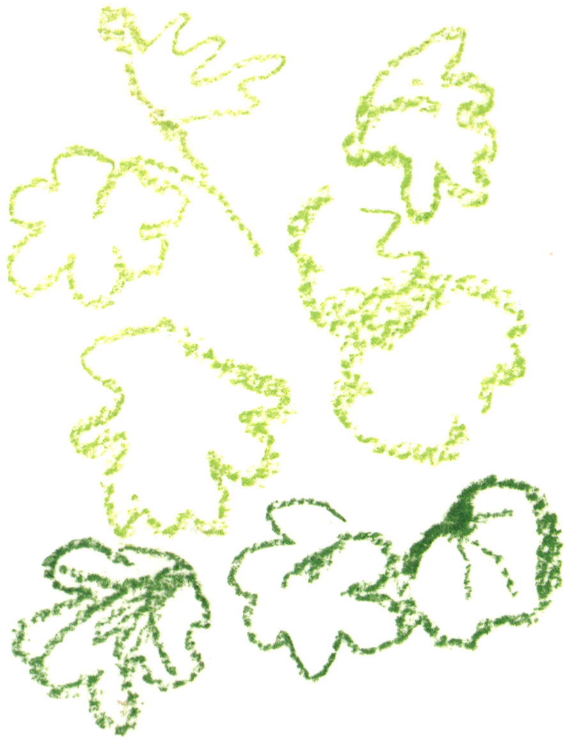

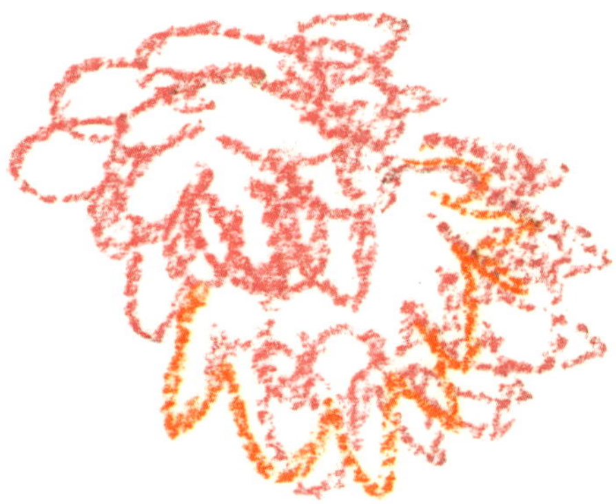

Geranium flower-heads are also irregular, with their clusters of round petals. Remembering the use of a scribble to make delphinium flower-heads in Project 1, use the same light touch to make clusters of circles, without ever putting the pastel down on the paper too heavily.

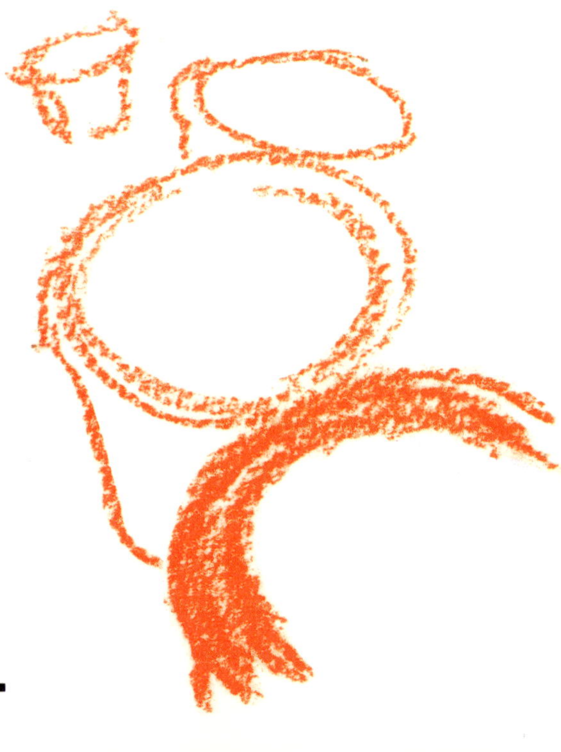

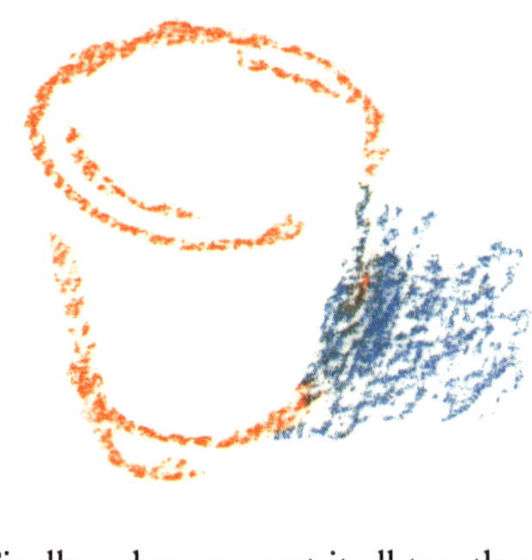

Finally, when you put it all together, the very light blue shadow area gives just the depth required to make the whole drawing pull together. Note that you only see one stem go down to the soil – it is enough to hint at the facts; you don't have to repeat them.

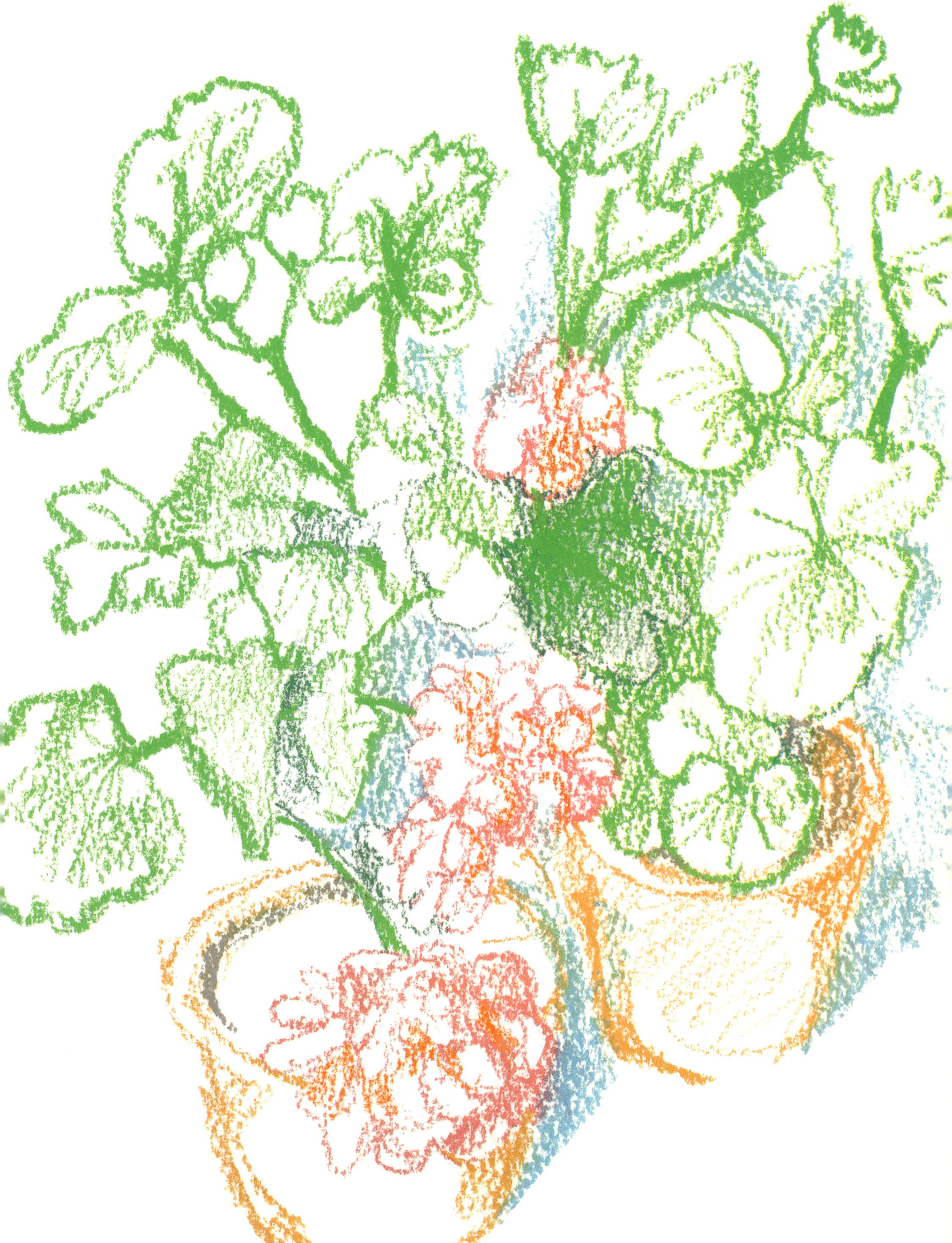

PART FIVE: BLENDING

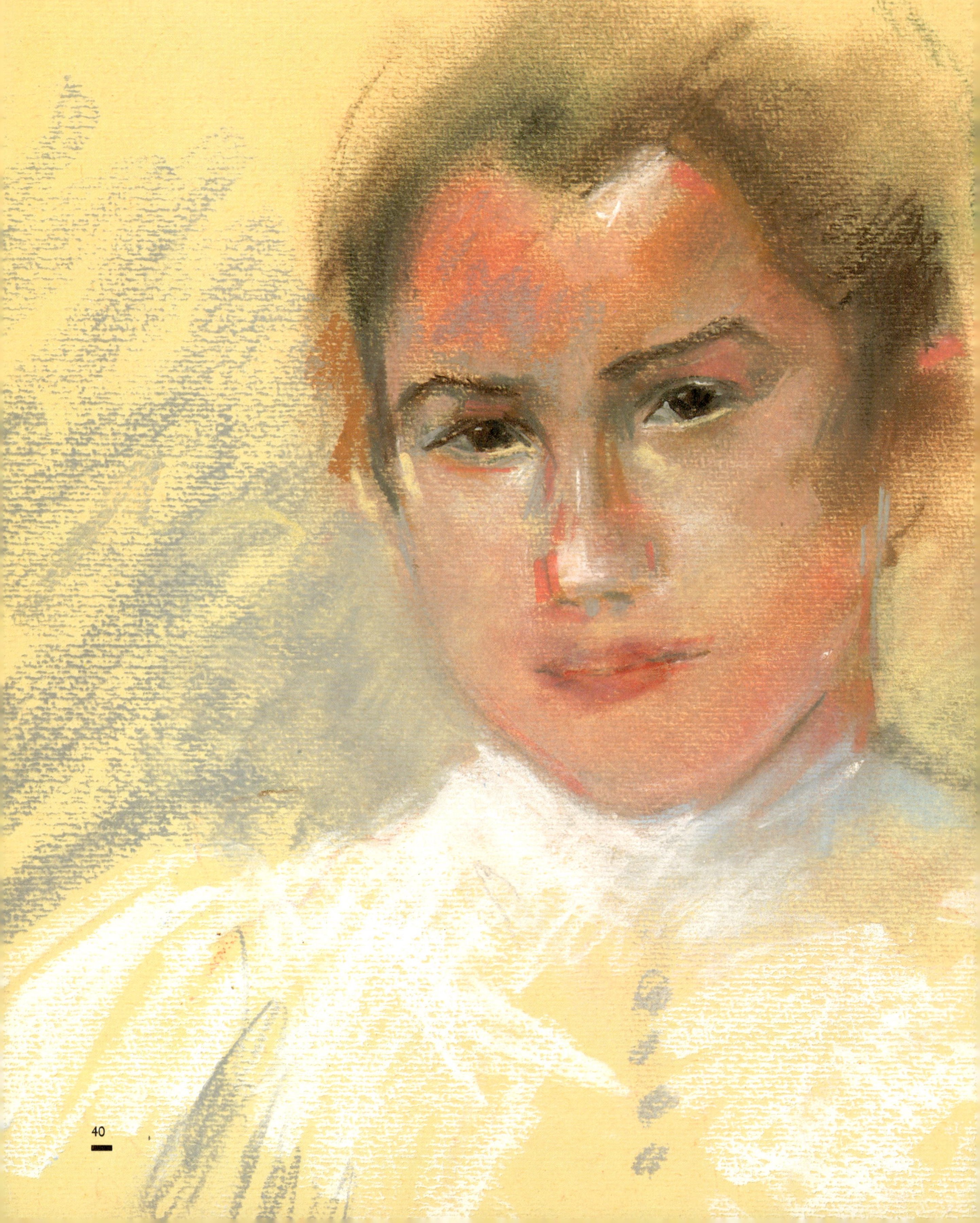

Since the days of Fragonard, the 'bloom' that soft pastels create when they are blended carefully has been highly prized. The smooth texture of a cheek, a plum, a knot of hair – all add immeasurably to the charm of eighteenth-century pictures.

Today a few portrait artists still work in such delicate tones, but even for the beginner the technique of blending various colours should not be forgotten.

Just one section of an image can be blended, and you can use as few as two or three colours, or as many as twenty.

Generally speaking, the soft traditional pastels blend most effectively. While oil or wax pastels will blend in small areas, they are difficult to work, and there will often be a slight thickening of the surface and streaks of the different colours.

Properly blended colours should change gradually and imperceptibly, so that you see a soft mutation rather than thick, crunchy bands of related tones.

The only tools you need are your fingers. The technique is a very careful, circular smudging, but because there is more than one colour involved, you may have to work the pastels with greater pressure, and it will certainly take more time.

Eventually the surface of the paper should be covered in a smooth sheen. Blending is a very tactile technique and a valuable addition to your skills.

Project 13 Working In

Birch Tree

Out walking one day, I saw a birch tree at the edge of a wood, its leaves dark green on one side, touched with sunshine on the other. But in the centre, the grey trunk looked curiously separate from the rest of the tree. I immediately decided to make a sketch that would emphasize that curious effect.

'Working in' describes the start of blending, when you are getting used to the technique of using just enough pressure to break up the tiny particles of two colours and mix them thoroughly so that they blend into one another.

Begin by drawing a few trunk-like shapes and, using just two tones of grey and the tips of your fingers, model the shape of the bumps and clefts on the trunk until the colours blend into each other. There should be no precise point where the light and dark separate.

You will learn to feel the changes in your fingers; feeling the trunk grow round as you blend in the shadows; feeling where the base of the branches begins as you model their shape with shades of colour.

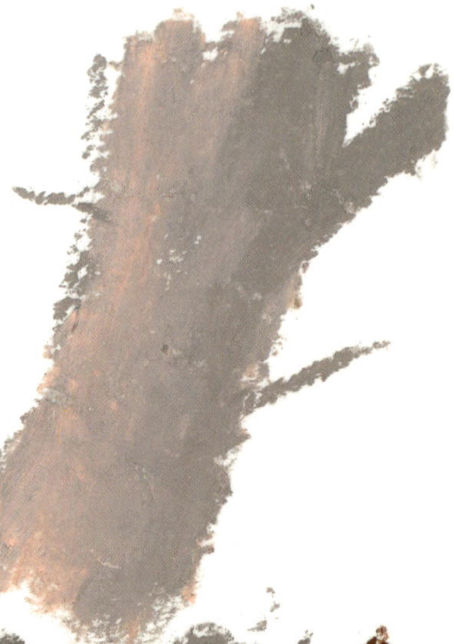

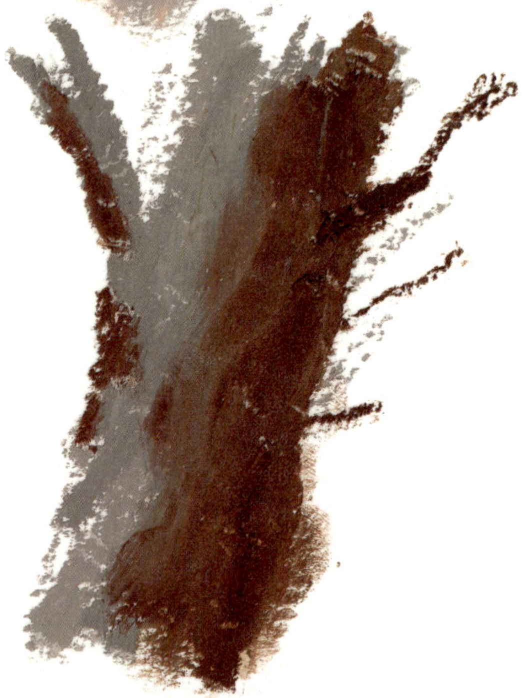

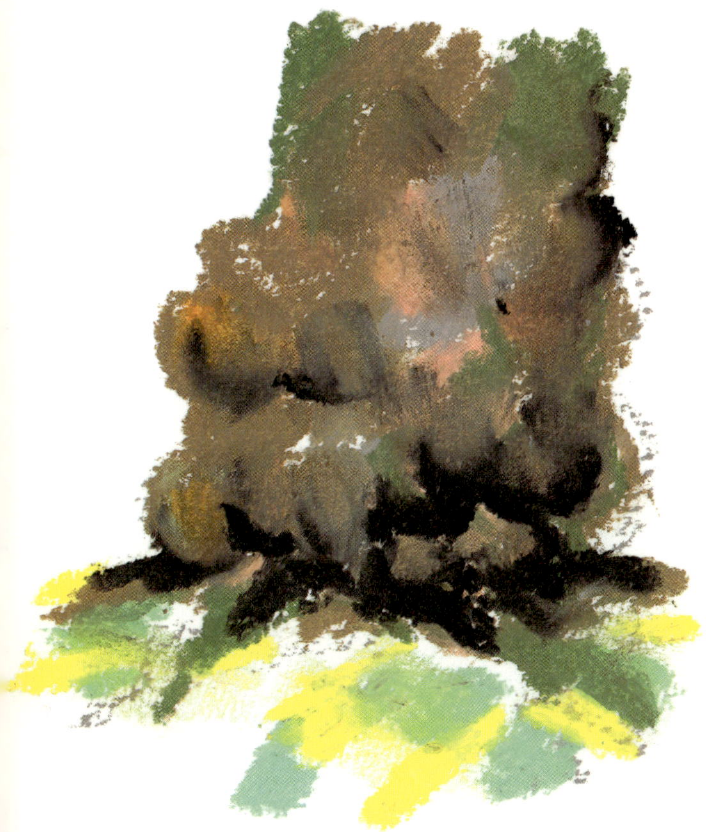

When you are ready to work on the final sketch, don't forget to keep the lighter-coloured leaves on one side to help the modelling. You are going to have very smudgy fingers, and keeping them off the rest of the paper is a priority! Wash your hands often, so that there is no build-up of pastel dust on your palms and wrists that might be transferred to your face and irritate your eyes.

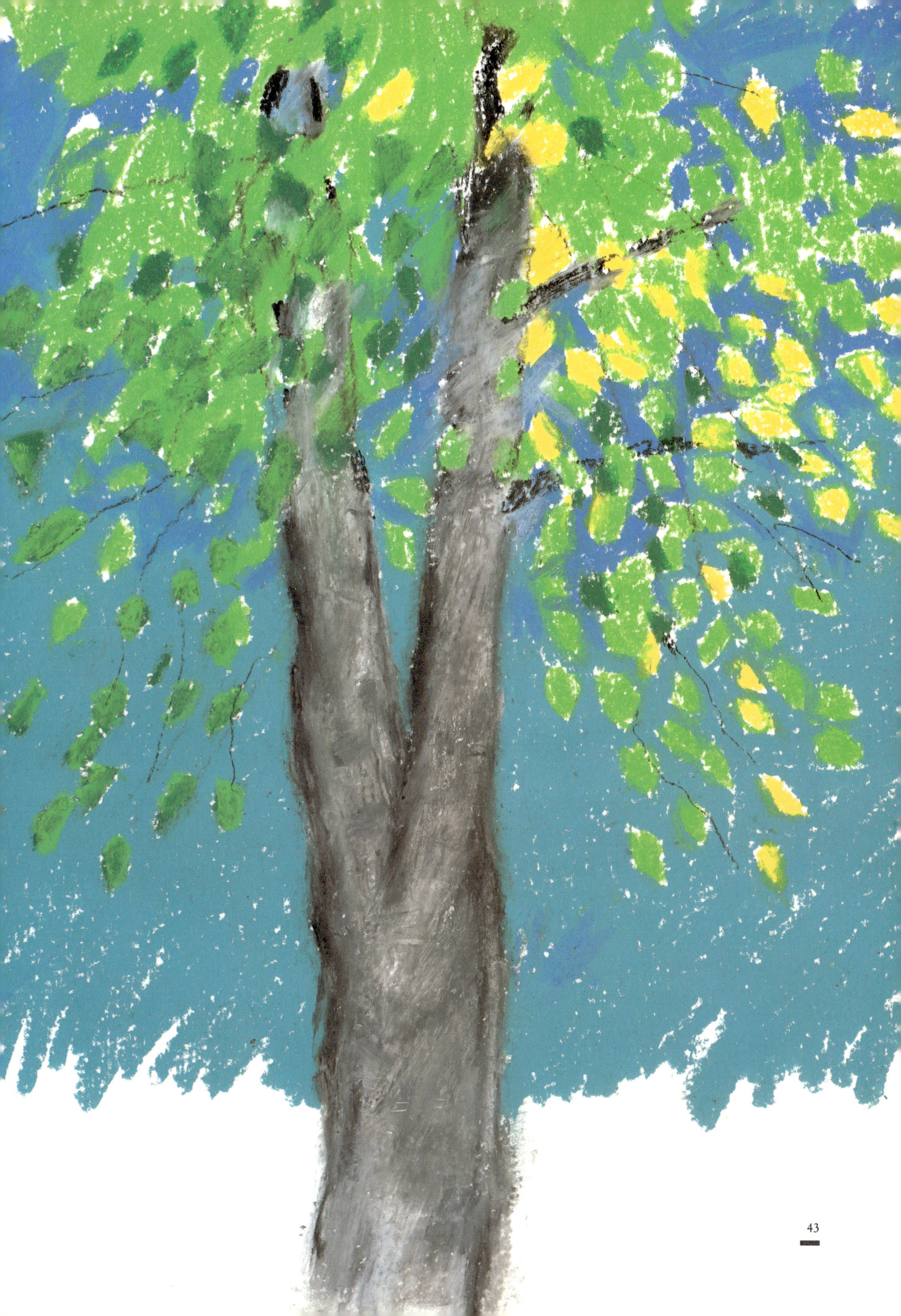

First Portrait

This simple portrait began with a soft pink oval for the face, light brown hair and a matching sweater. My reluctant model (a neighbour who would rather have been finishing her shopping) was watching uneasily to see how long I was going to take.

Start by making an oval in the lightest pink in your box. Don't even think about the features, just use your little finger to spread soft colour over the entire area.

Add a light ochre over the cheeks, the chin, and the eye sockets. Now blend this in, without moving too far outside the area you want to model. One of the secrets of blending is to keep the colour where you want it. That means using your little finger, the edge of your finger and, for very small details, a cotton-tipped stick or a flat-ended brush. Try them all on repeated pink ovals, and see which you prefer.

Once you are comfortable with the technique, you can add the lines for eyes and mouth on top of the blended areas. Make a few brown strokes for hair and sweater, blending them very quickly and lightly, then put in a few deep crease-marks and so on, where necessary, to shape the image.

In this first study I have left the crease-marks without attempting to sink them into the background. It helps to keep the sketchy character of the portrait.

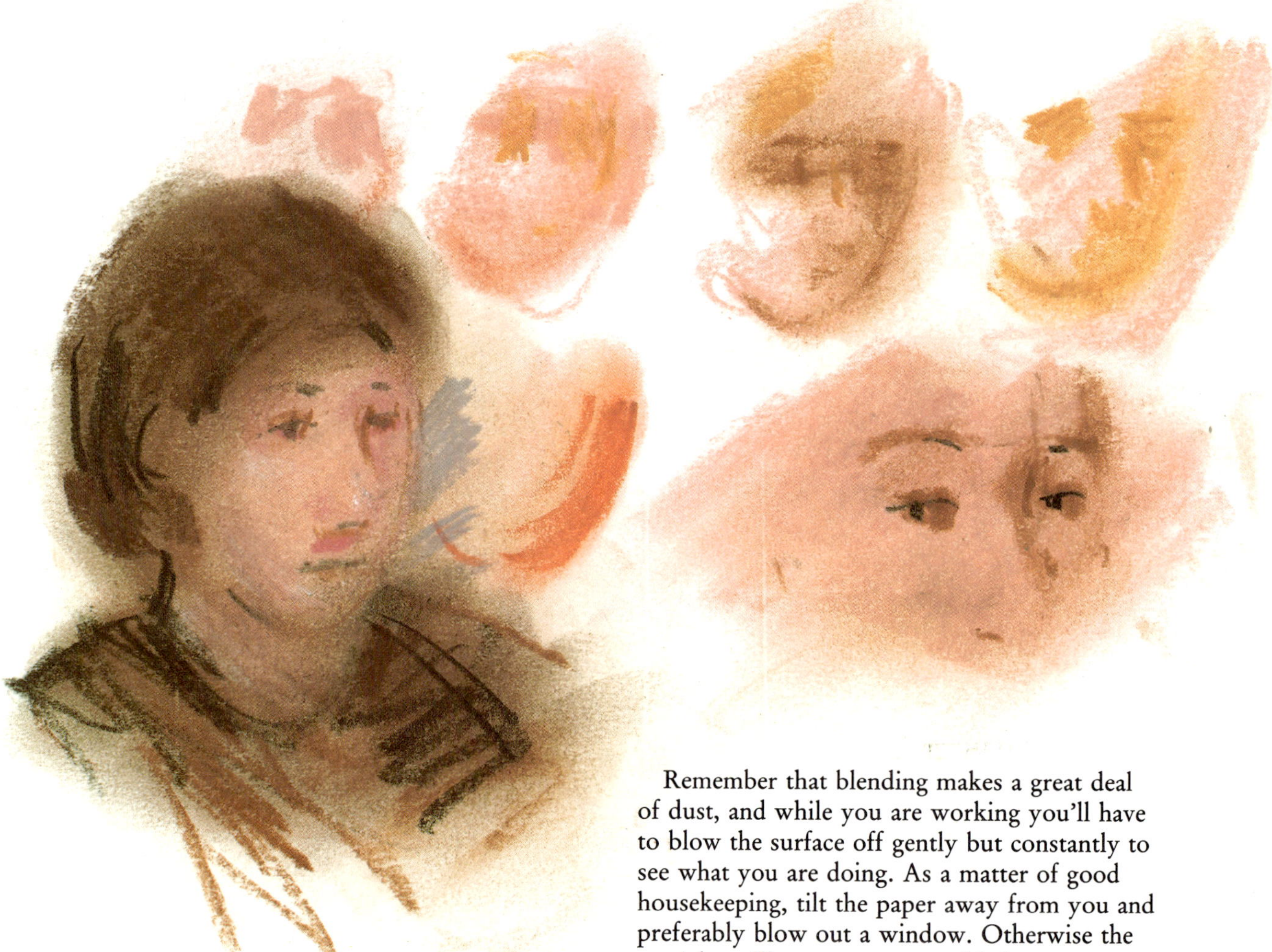

Remember that blending makes a great deal of dust, and while you are working you'll have to blow the surface off gently but constantly to see what you are doing. As a matter of good housekeeping, tilt the paper away from you and preferably blow out a window. Otherwise the particles will come to rest on fabrics, carpets, tabletops, even ceilings! If this is not possible, cover a reasonable area with newspaper.

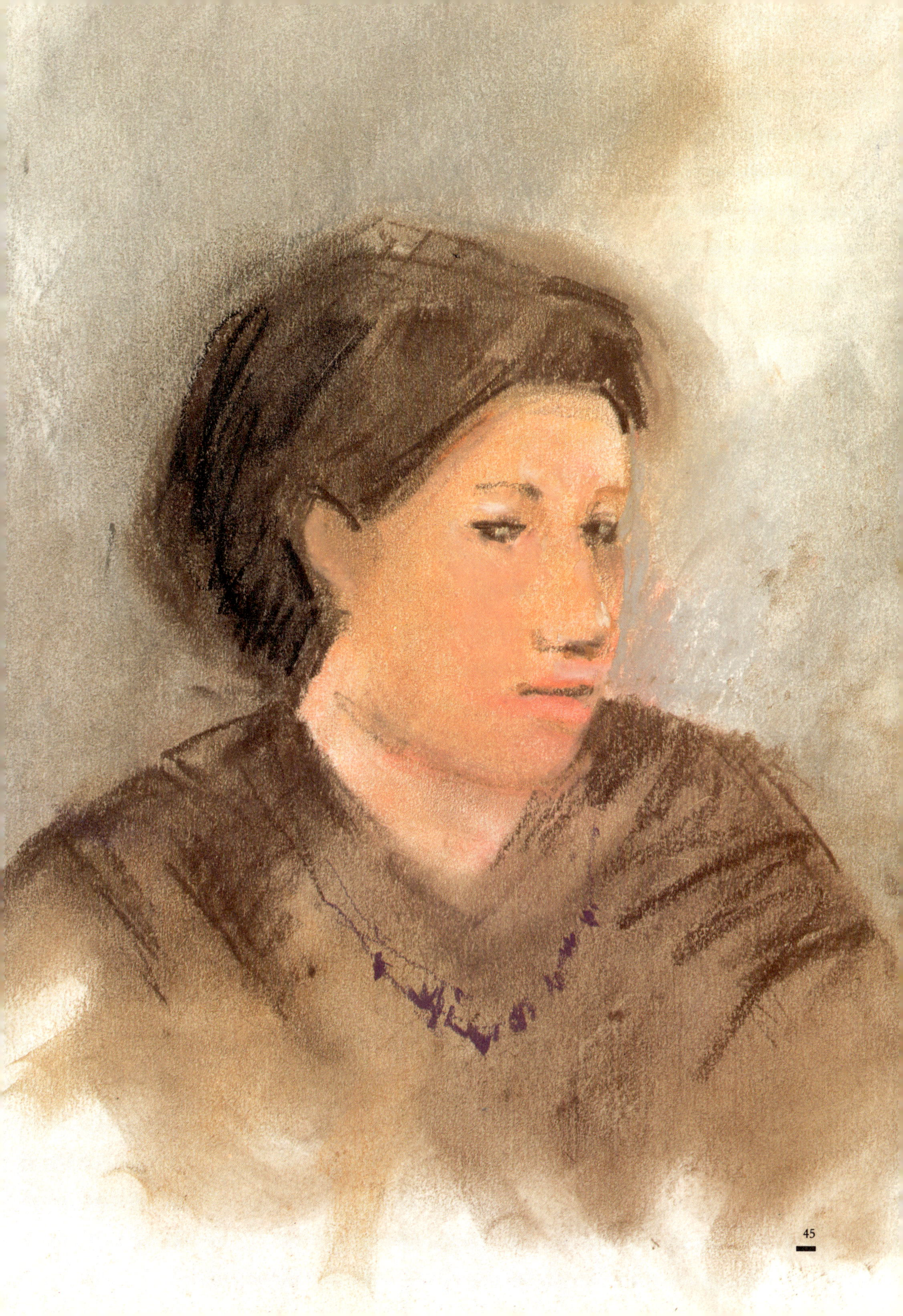

Project 15 All-Over Blending

Seated Model

When a picture is blended over most of its surface, the entire image changes. It will have a smooth sheen, and even modelling shadows will be blended in an indistinct shift of colour.

Basic colours are laid on, with the light tints being put down first. Then gradually darker tints and shadows are added until you have the effect you want.

Practise blending a busy pattern; start with tiny blocks of colour in pinks, greens, reds, whatever you wish. For the first trial, use a blurred pattern like my model is wearing, without any definition. Later, as you grow more confident, you can try out larger patterns with definite designs, like ribbons or hazy stripes or flower-heads.

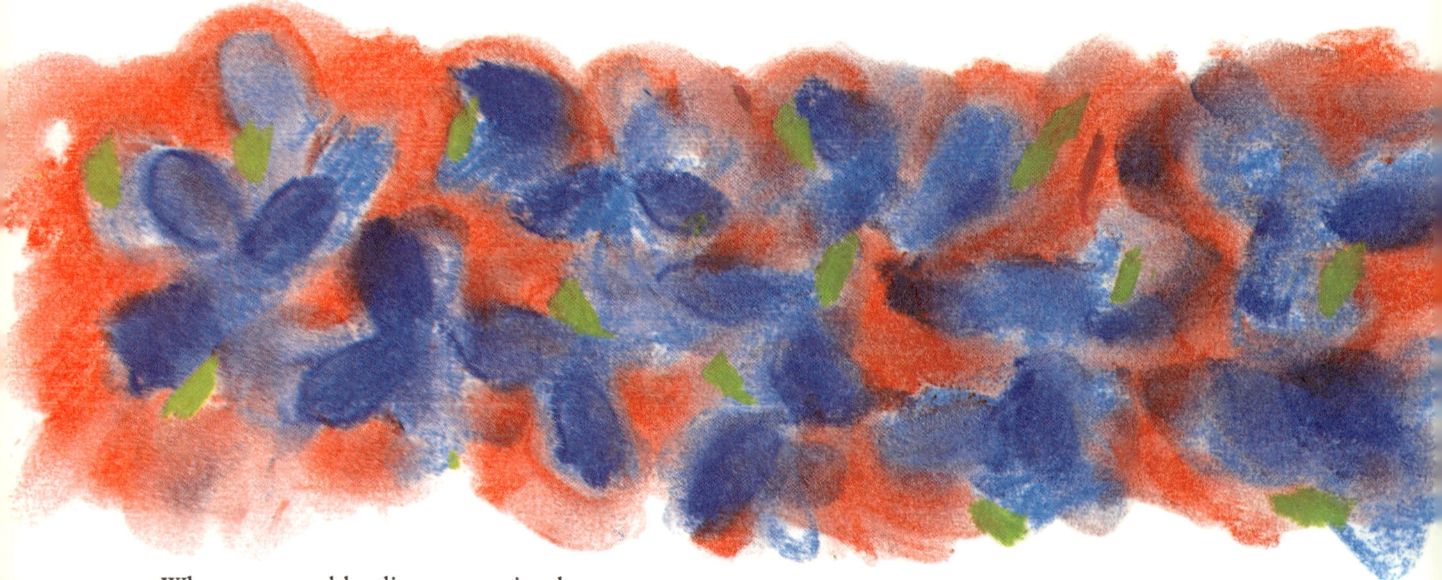

When you are blending, use a circular motion so that the different flecks of colour are amalgamated into a single whole. Larger blended circles follow the line of drawing and mould the colour – look at the knot of hair at the back of the model's head.

To round the shapes you will need to keep adding touches of shadow and working them in wherever you need them. Watch the edges of the drawings – you want to keep the outline of the cheek crisp, for example, so blending has to stop just short of the line. The sharper spectacle frame helps to define the line of her face.

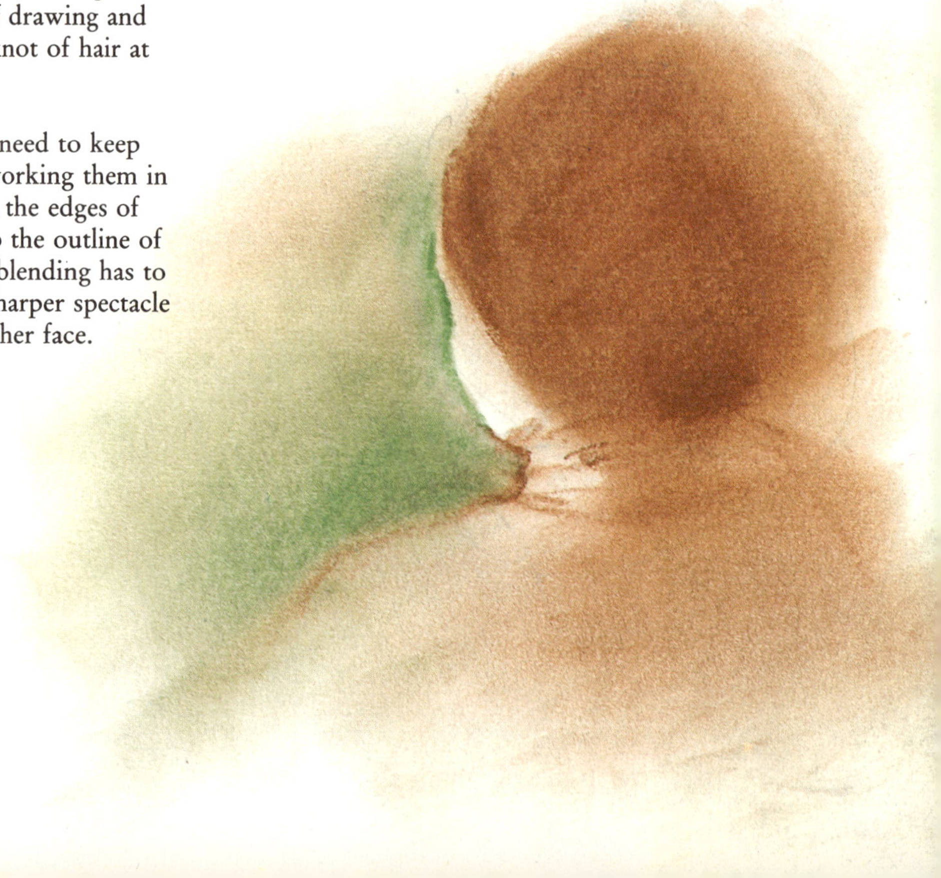

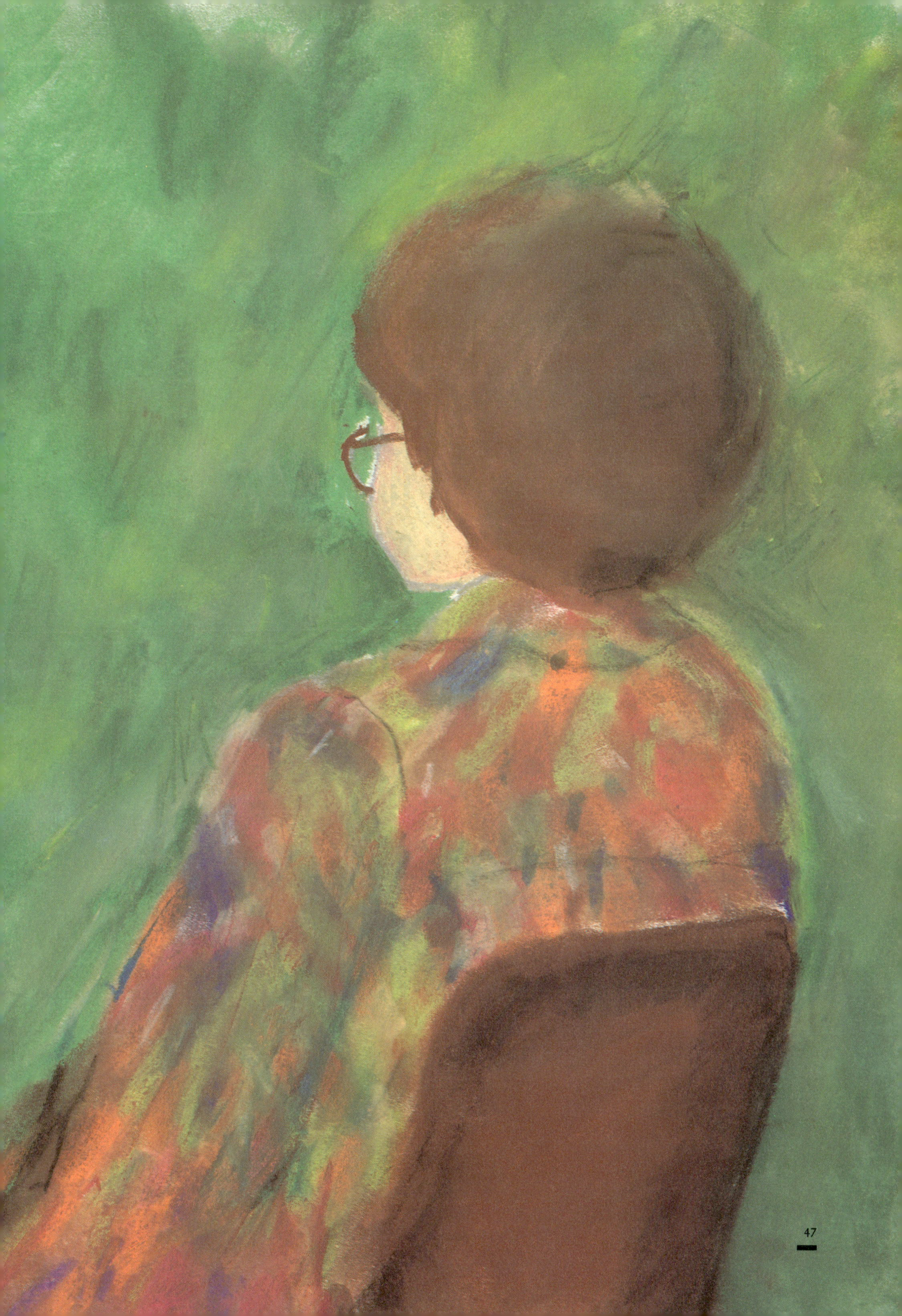

PART SIX: TINTED PAPER

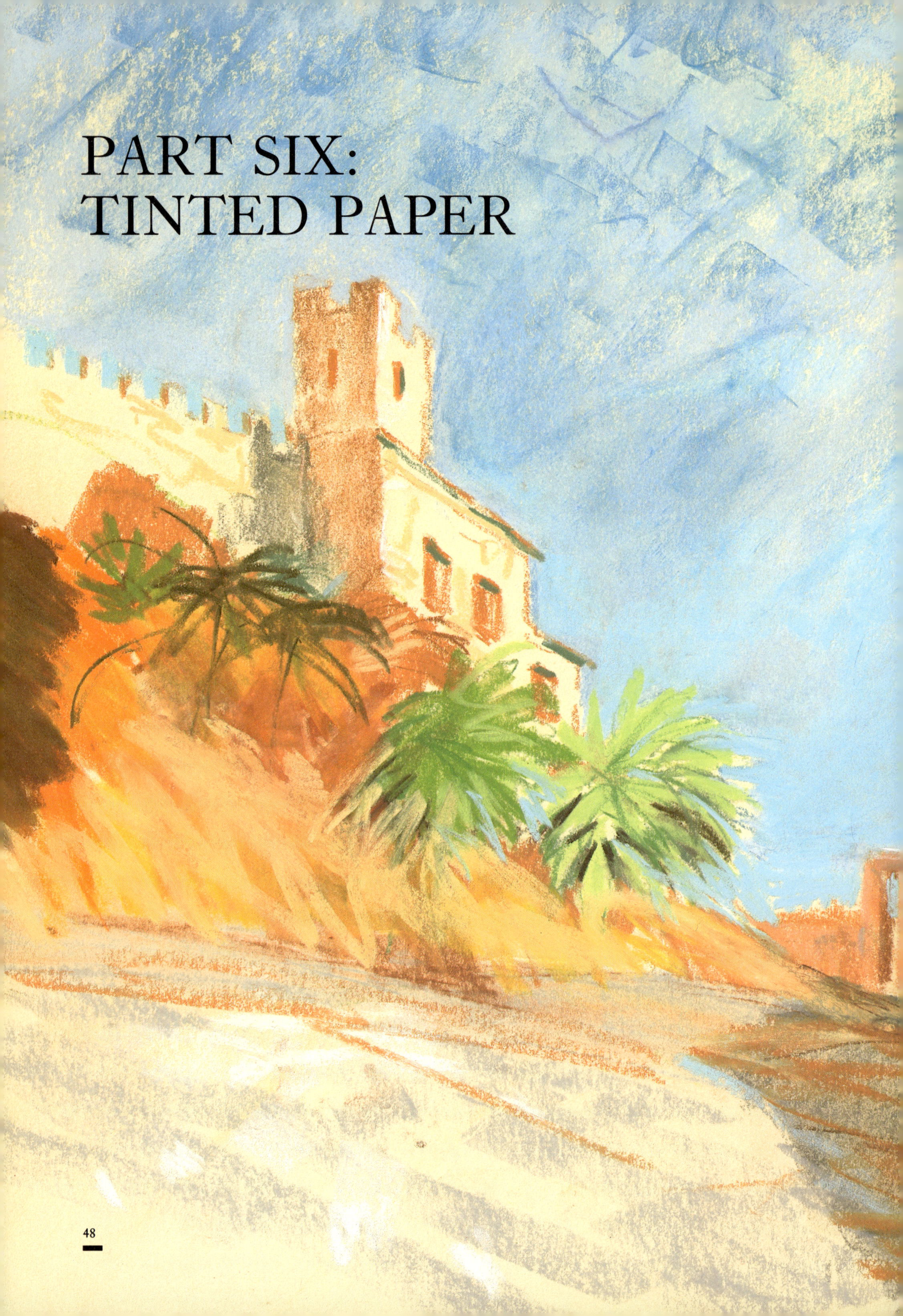

Many pastel artists use tinted paper almost exclusively. I do use white paper most of the time, but there are times when only a coloured background will do the subject justice.

In addition, by linking the colour of the paper to a colour you want to use in the drawing, you can let tint and texture become part of the picture, in the same way that you let white paper show through as highlights.

Ingres paper, popularized by the French artists of the nineteenth century, is now the easiest tinted paper to find, and it comes in a very wide variety. The made-up pads do tend to stick to conventional blues, greys and beiges, but there are more colours available in open stock, which you can buy by the sheet.

However, why not look for other sources? Plain brown card, used for the back of many paper pads, offers a very interesting texture. Most art shops have a number of different papers, varied not only in weight but in tone. Almost always they will have a few deep, dramatic colours, often intended for posters or mounts.

Avoid papers where the texture is too rough; the pastel sticks will miss so much of the surface that your image may break up entirely. Other than that, try everything – you may come upon the perfect combination of surface, texture and colour, purely by chance!

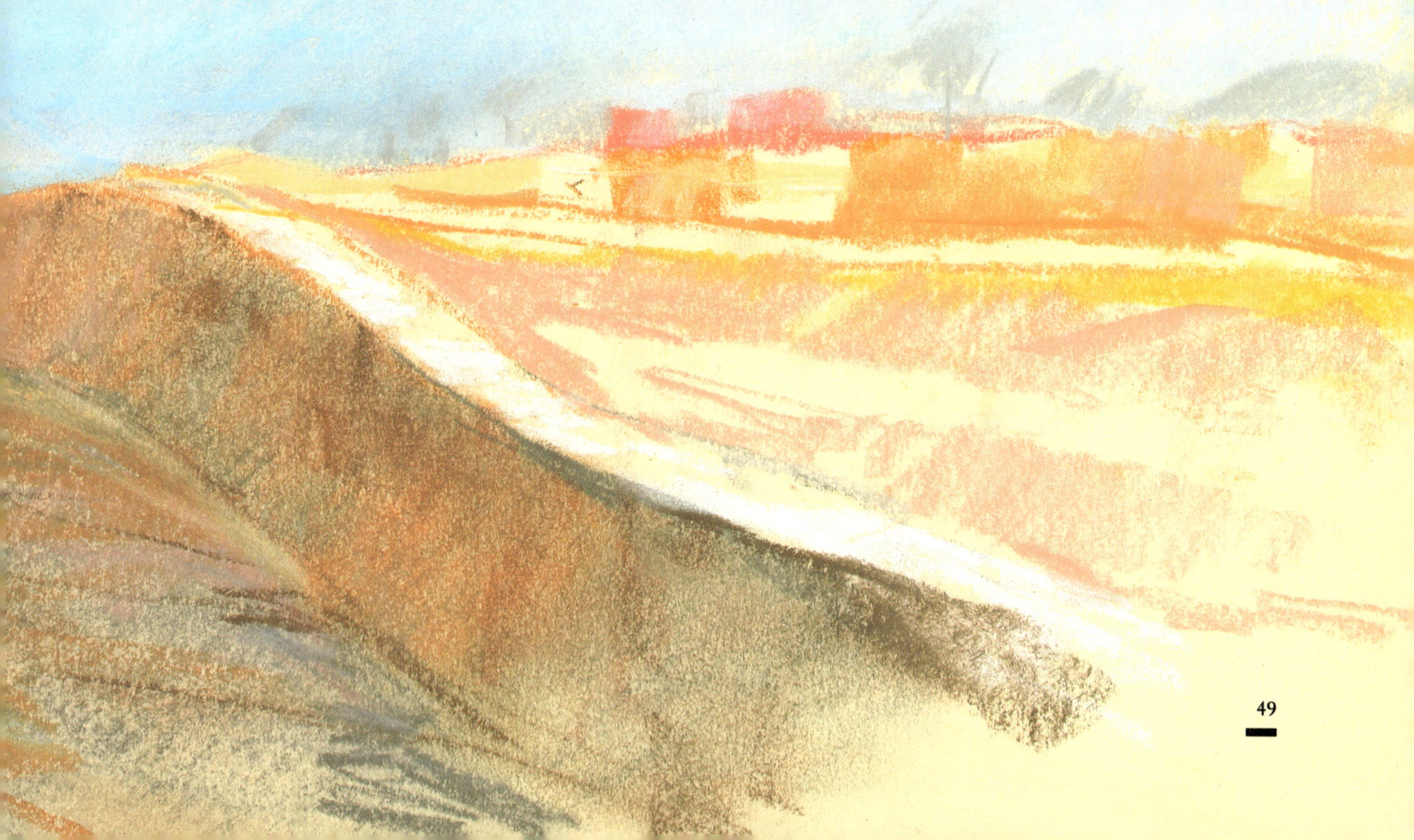

Flower Pots

I have said that when you are working with tinted papers you should try and find a colour that suits your subject. At first it would seem that blue-grey was not particularly appropriate for a study of flower pots. Why not terracotta, or green?

But the pots didn't really attract me; I saw instead the heavy texture of the wooden shelf on which they were sitting. Years of exposure had weathered the original surface, and it had a soft colour, almost identical to an Ingres paper in my pad.

I laid the paper over the actual wood, and rubbed a pastel stick across it, as if I were doing a brass rubbing. The result was a wonderful sweep of graining. When you find a surface with such texture and character, try the same technique.

Lay the paper directly on top, hold it firmly and sweep across the whole paper with as large a stick of soft pastel as you have in your box. Be very careful to keep the paper still – if it moves around you'll find that the pattern becomes broken and loses its appeal.

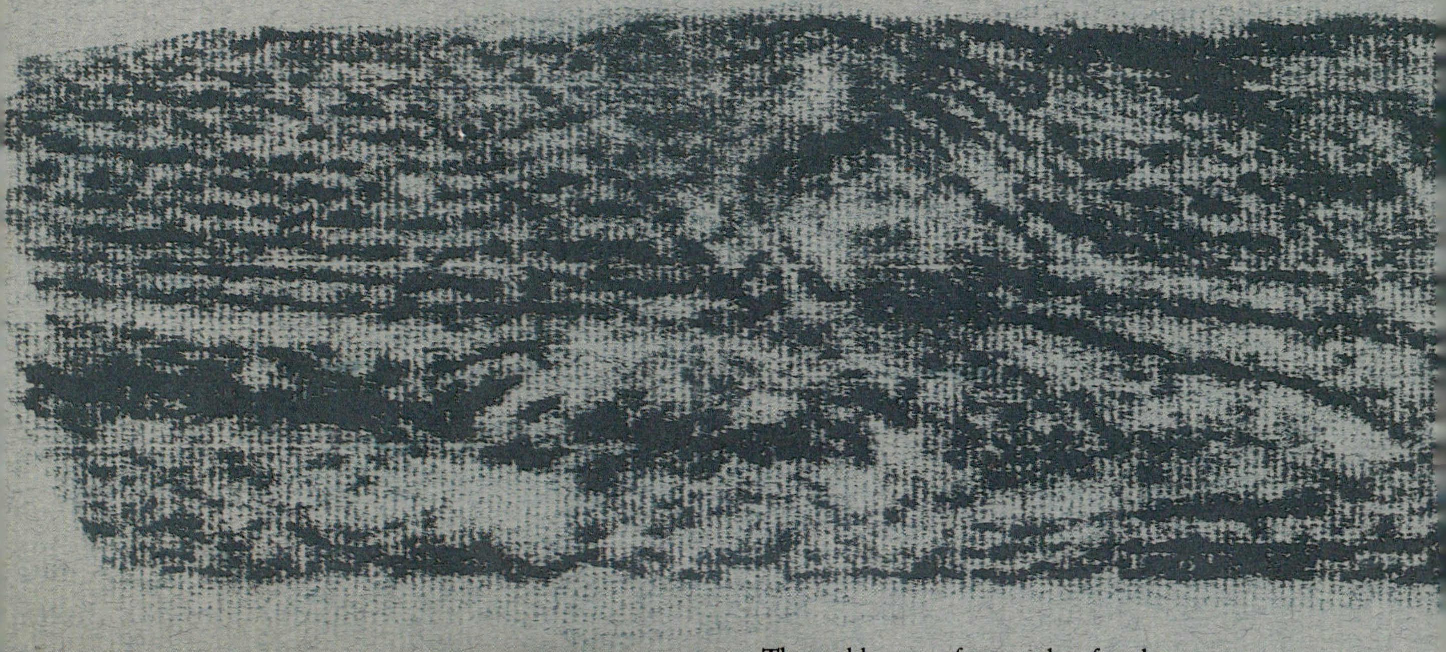

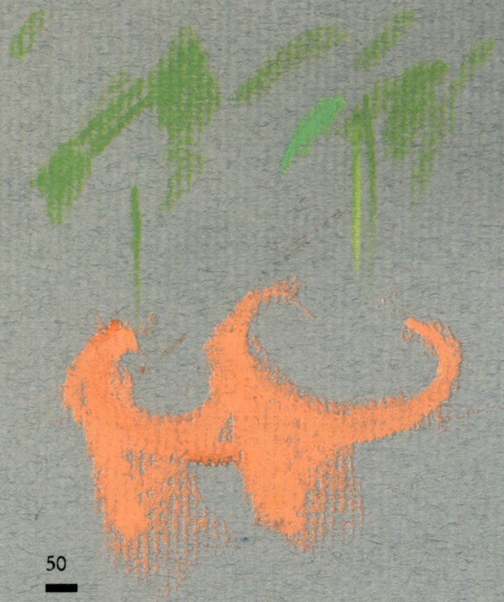

Then add a very few strokes for the pots and the leaves. Make sure they are done on a smooth surface, so that you get not only the colour but the variation in texture as well.

You can try all kinds of surfaces; woven cane will give an interesting pattern, so will flock wallpaper, embossed lettering, and so on.

There is no need to keep to an appropriate colour, either. This wood graining might look equally attractive as a yellow wall, or the blue rippling of shallow water. Let your mind roam!

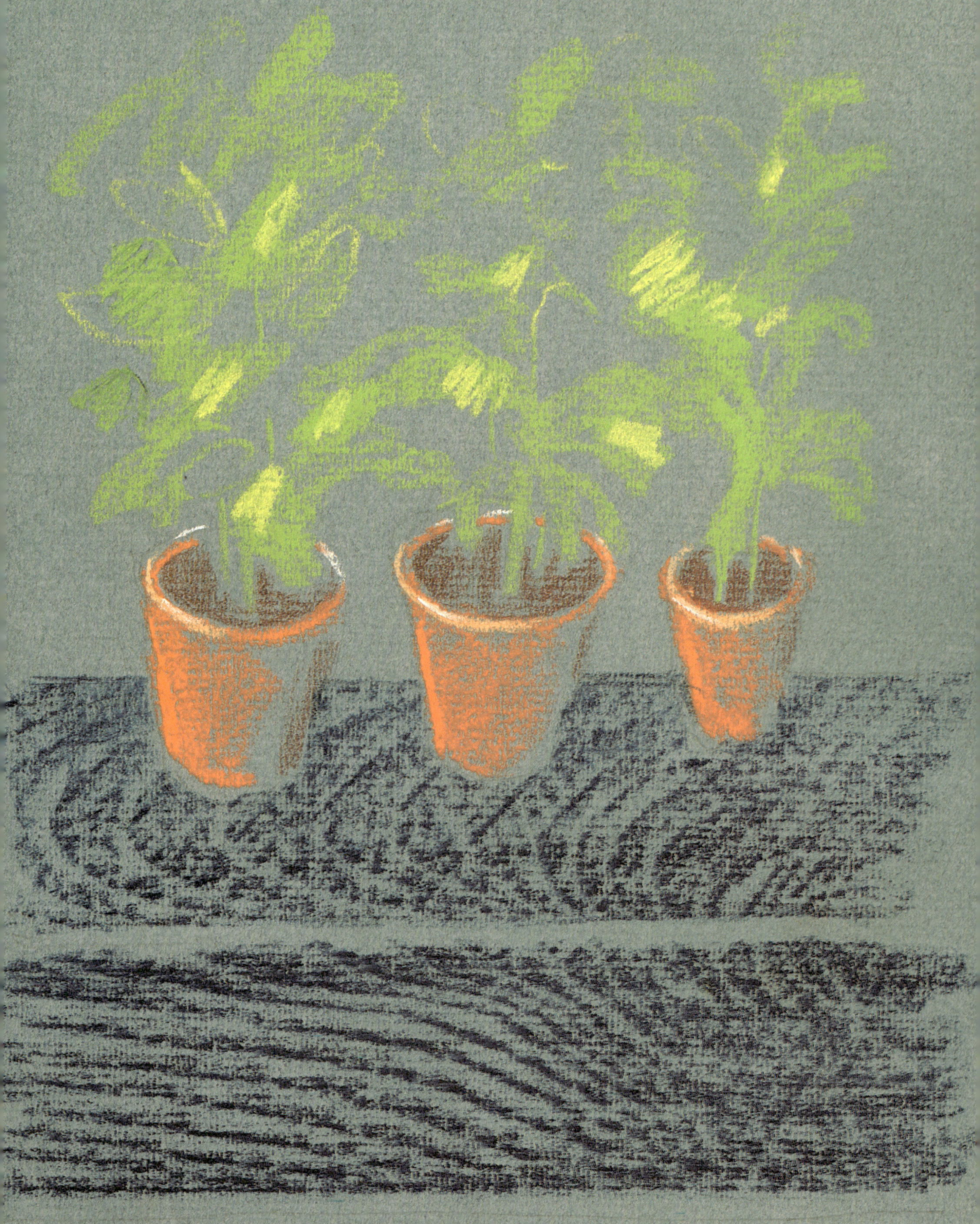

Project 17 Minimal Texture

Baby Owl

A traditional Ingres paper was the starting point for this picture. The result I wanted was in direct contrast to the previous project: as little colour or pattern as possible.

Pastel is almost unique in being able to look really soft and fluffy, because of its own dusty composition. Nothing more than a little circle of white is needed to make this owl. Rub across a circle with your white stick, used very lightly indeed. Blend in from the centre, and let the edges become even lighter. But don't go outside the circle, or you will ruin the illusion. You need to make only very small, light circular motions with your little finger, or use a cotton-tipped stick.

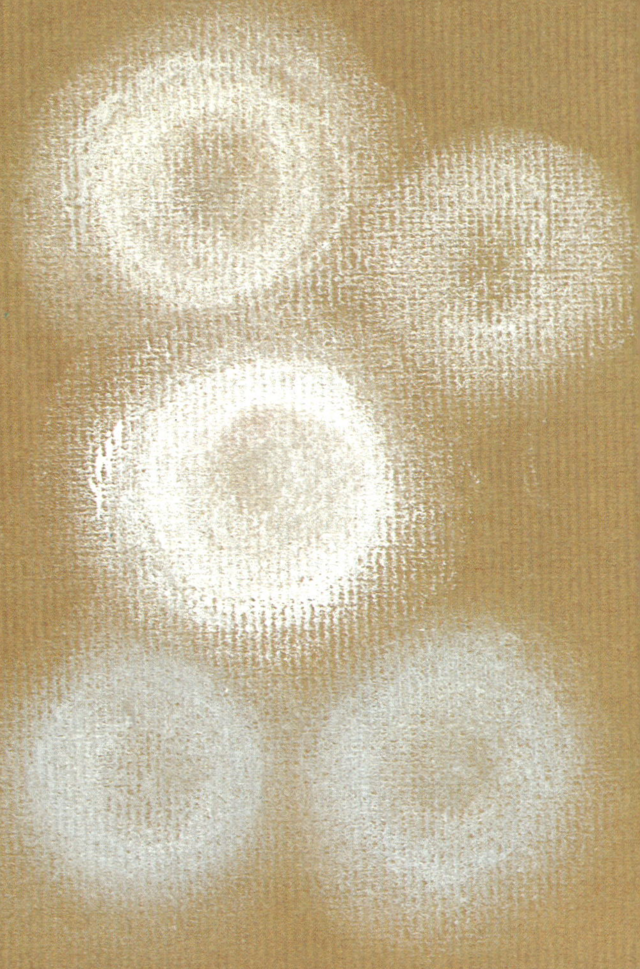

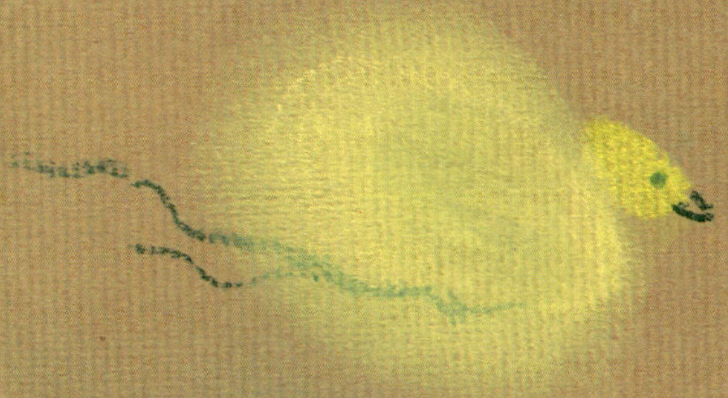

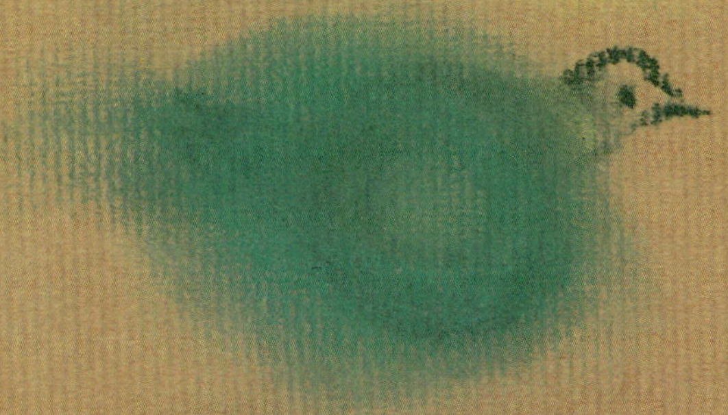

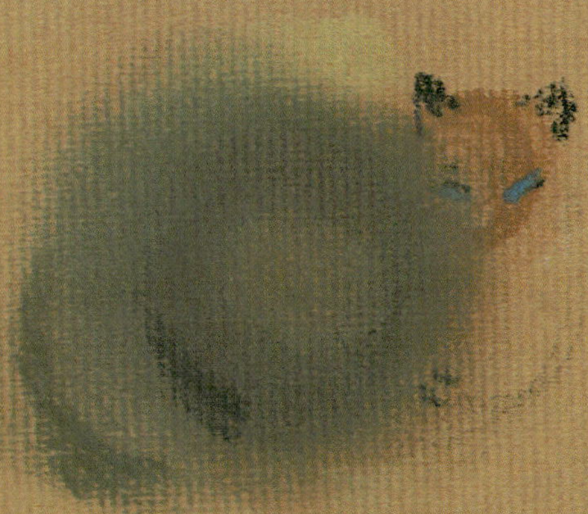

Blow off any surplus before you continue, so that you can see exactly where you are going to put the few extra touches. Look for the outstanding features of eyes, eyebrows and beak, and touch them in very lightly. Spray the picture with fixative and let it dry. Only then add the claws and the branch to balance the image, and finally fix it again.

A few words of warning. Making a miniature like this depends on the illusion of fragility and light. I saw an owl in my white pastel circle; you might see a kitten or a gosling. If you change the subject, choose your colours with the same light touch. If you have a yellow duckling, for example, use a gold paper; for a blue-eyed kitten use a blue-grey paper; and so on. Don't use a dramatic, dark paper, and don't try to repeat the image on a large scale. It's unlikely to work.

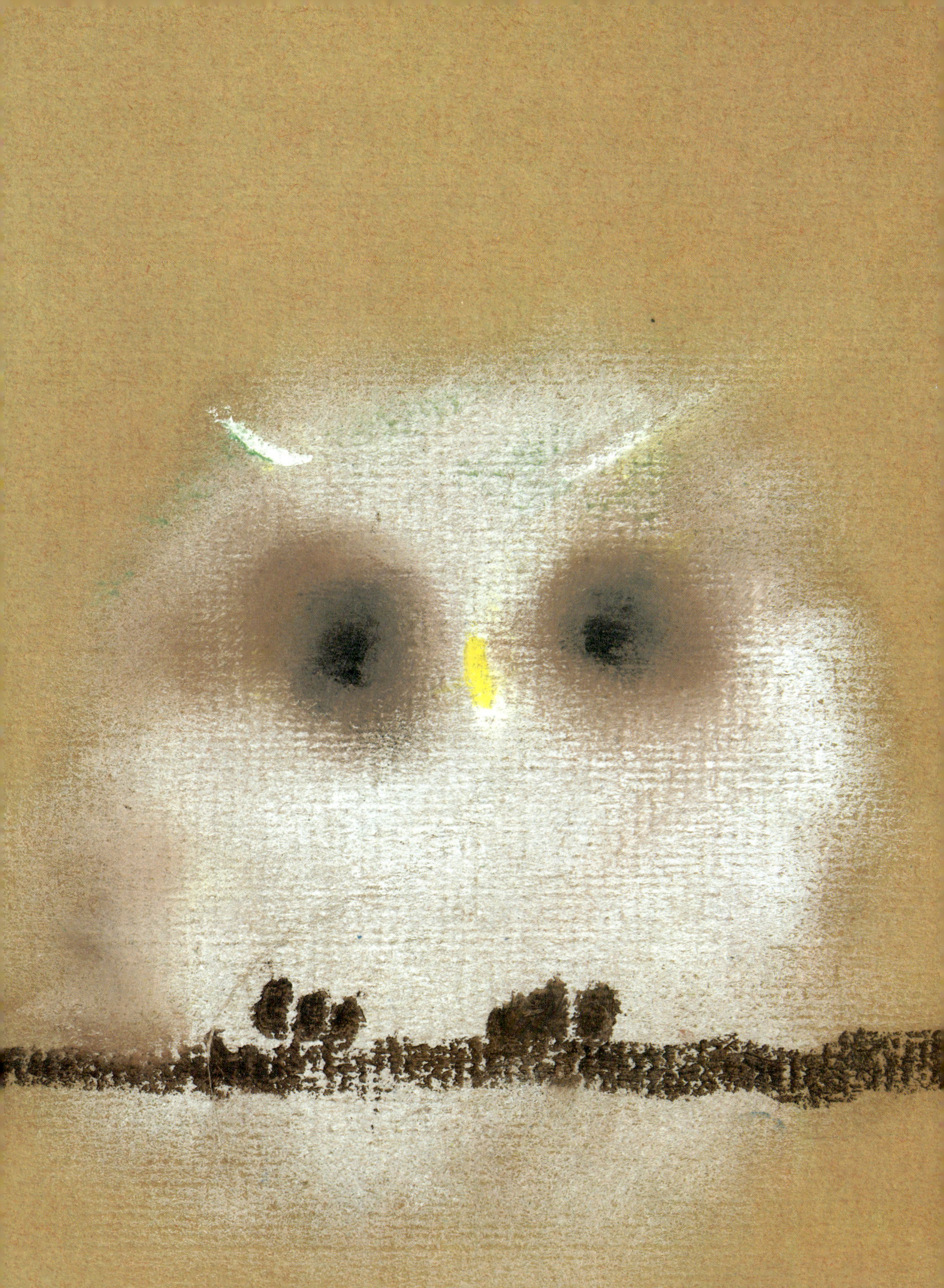

Still Life with Fruit

This project used light mushroom-tinted paper as underpainting, rather than to make a strong statement. The tone of the Ingres paper adds warmth and depth to everything on the table; even the white highlights have an extra glow of peach, and the orange background looks sunny instead of harsh, as it would on a pure white paper.

The bowl of fruit and its contents work with the tinted paper to display another technique – the images are modelled with fairly distinct bands of colour instead of blended shadows.

Begin with the bowl; the basic colour is blue, and the light is coming from the right. I used a pale grey for the lightest part, but you could also use a very pale blue. Block in the variation from left and right with strong strokes of lighter and darker colour.

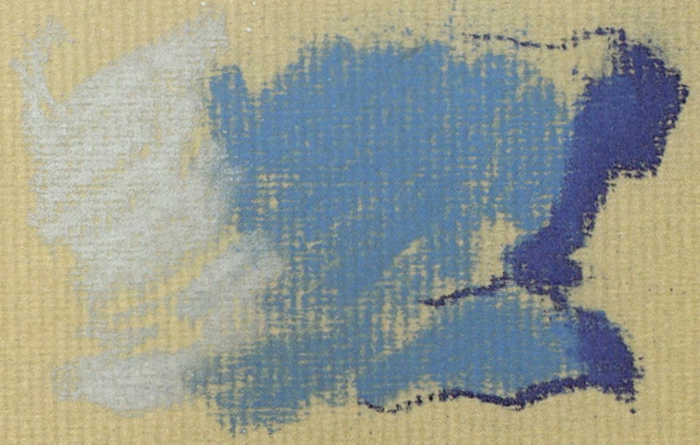

Do the same with shapes of bananas, with apples, or with any other fruit you are using as models. The dark shadows under the bananas were blocked in quite flatly with strokes of brown, and the tablecloth was laid down with stripes that do not diminish as they recede from your eye.

Yet in spite of that, if you stand well back from your sketch, the immediate impression will be quite three-dimensional. Colours modulate the shapes, and the tinted paper helps a great deal by unifying the colours with its softness. Try the same exercise on white paper and see how much sharper the result will be.

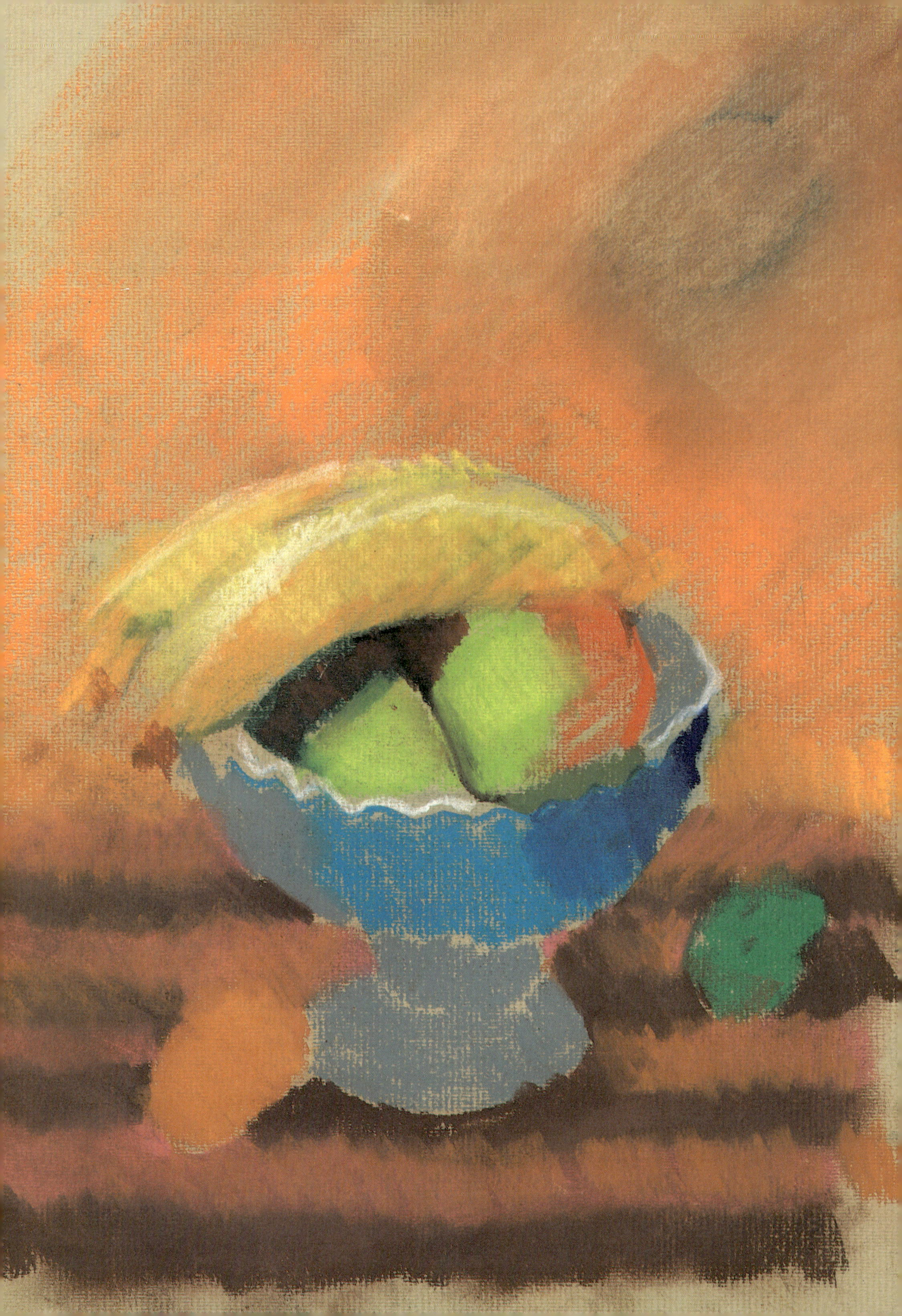

PART SEVEN: MORE ABOUT TINTS

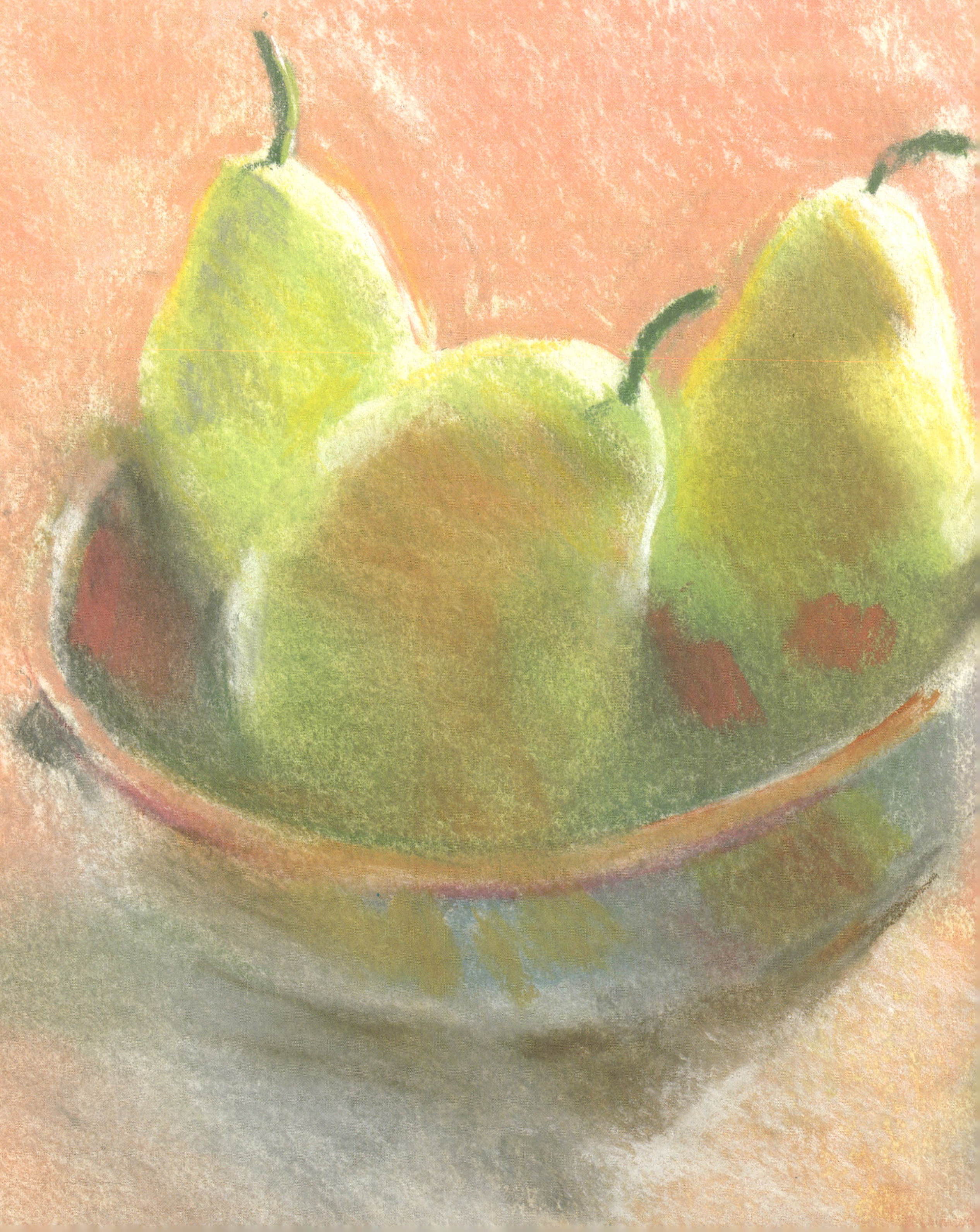

Tinted and blended background colours can play a part far beyond the obvious; because soft pastel is usually such an open-textured medium, the background is even more important than it is in watercolour or oil paintings.

To take real advantage of this attribute of the medium, and to give your pictures added interest and variety, you will need to make a paper guide. This will prove very useful when you are considering what background colour to use for any one project.

Ingres paper is, as I have said, the most common kind of tinted pastel paper. When you buy your first pad, make a notebook by cutting off a few inches of paper from every individual colour. There are usually about eight or nine different shades.

Stick the strips lightly to one piece of card, and then work over the different colours with your five or six favourite pastel colours. With an entire sheet of each Ingres tint you can make a chart using every pastel colour in your box! See p. 90 for further details.

Pin the papers up on the wall for quick reference when you are starting a new picture. A corresponding sheet of white paper pinned up by the side will give you a working comparison. Add sheets of new tints as you find them, and you will soon have a valuable resource that will add quality and variety to your work.

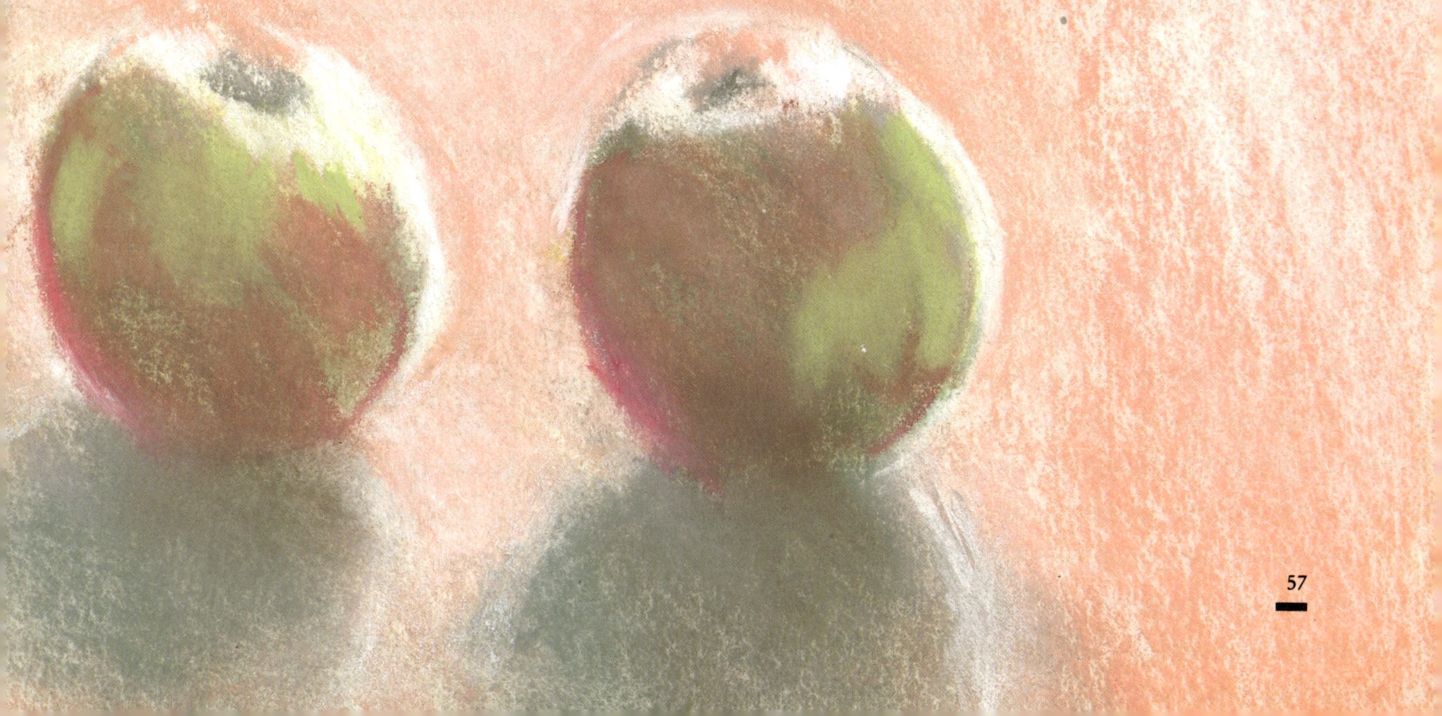

Beach Scene

One of the clever things about using paper as part of the picture is that you have much less to draw, and you can concentrate on the details. This brown paper with its unusual pattern is the inside of a large envelope, and the colour happened to be a perfect representation of sand.

Beach figures are great fun to draw and very easy to do. Start with larger figures, until you get the knack. One chunk makes the torso, then smaller chunks sketch in arms, legs, with a dark smudge for hair. Heads are slanted across, rather than up and down. No blondes on this beach, but two new visitors have pink skins to add that little touch of colour!

A few smudges here and there for swimsuits, a line of white for the sunlight on top of the limbs, and they are finished. Try to vary the positions of arms and legs, but remember to keep the light in the same relative position.

Move away from the foreground by making the figures progressively smaller and lighter. When you are beginning, do try and draw complete little figures. Later, as you grow more confident, you can fill in with just a jumble of side-strokes and top strokes.

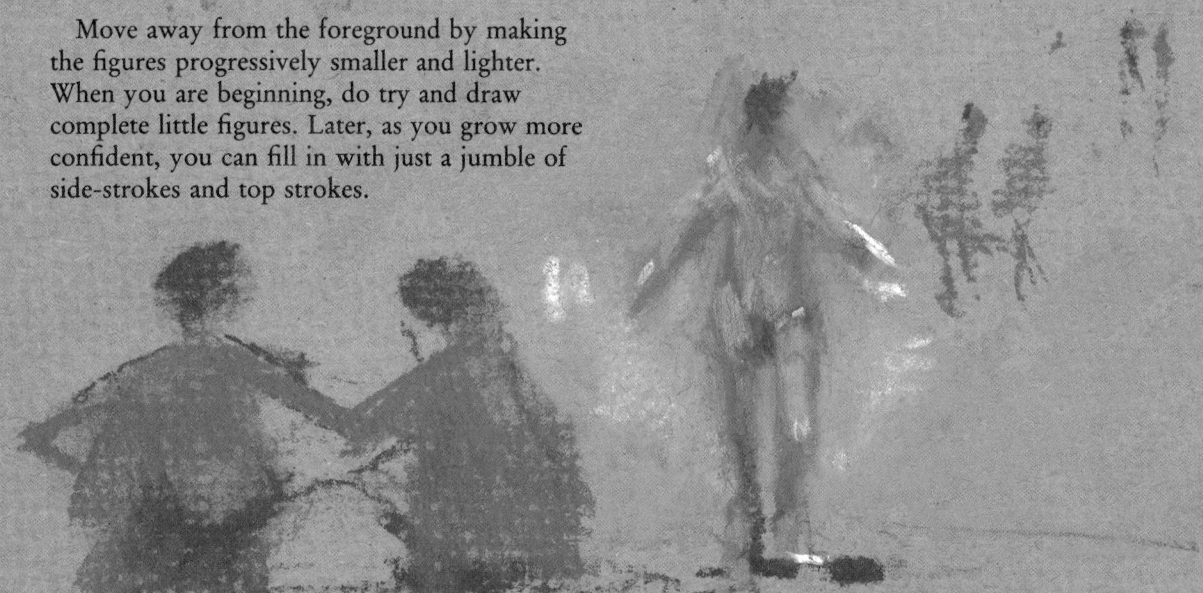

When you begin the final sketch, start with the sky; with so much of the background bare paper, you need to see the proportions of sky to ground. I did not make the sky very dark, because I knew there would be details later working themselves into the skyline.

The beach curved towards the eye, so I roughed in the lightest foam line at the edge of the sea, the lighter sand, and the slightly darker, nearer sand. These streaks of soft pastel can be blown off; they will leave just a faint 'snail trail' to show the structure of the scene.

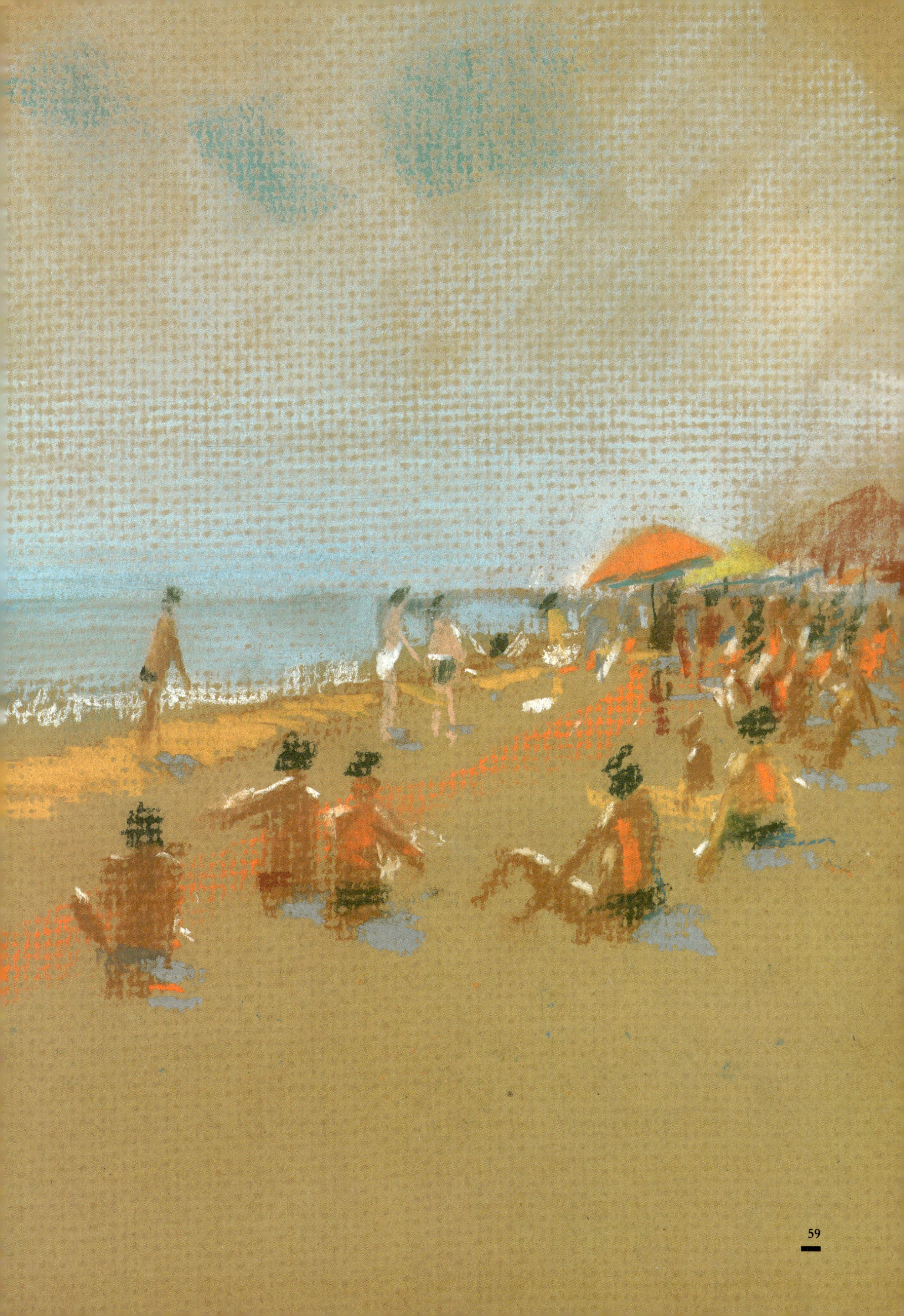

Roofs of Florence

When I discovered the tiny squared pattern on these envelopes, it became a real delight to find appropriate images and pictures. In the previous project, I used the envelope paper as part of the scene. Here I used it to create a constructional pattern on the walls of the buildings, giving them far more interest and surface tension than a flat paper would have done.

Play around with banks of windows. Try and keep them evenly spaced. Make a darker edge consistently either at the top or at one of the sides, to indicate the shadow.

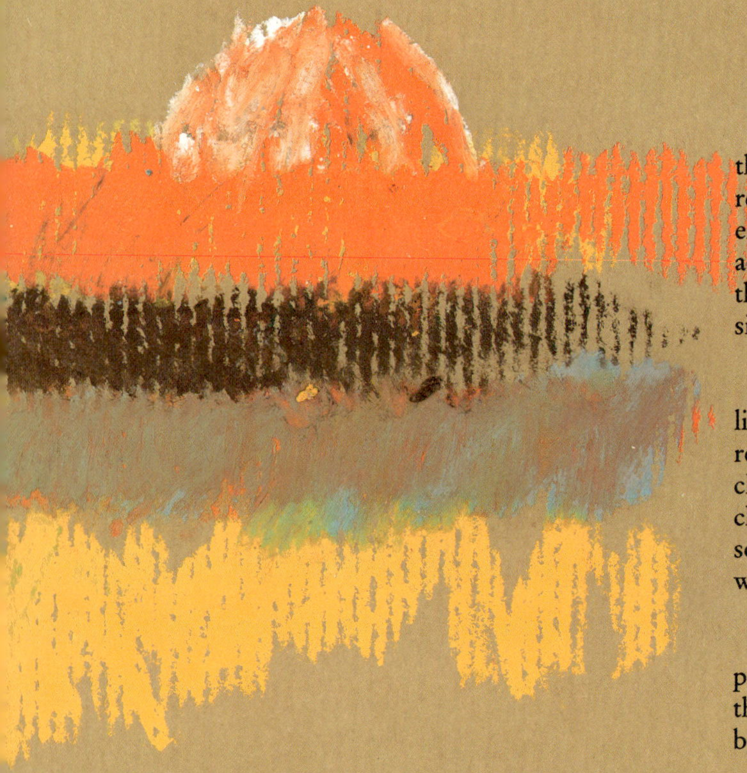

Roof views always look more complicated than they are. Try to half-close your eyes and reduce the picture to its simplest and strongest elements. In this case the sunlit embankment across the river formed the foundation, while the dome topped it off. In between, there were simply slabs of colour.

When you start the final sketch, put all the light colours down first, then use the orange roof lines to create horizontal streets, growing closer together as they climb towards the church. The roofs have to be firmly coloured, so they have no pattern – leave that for the walls.

Drawing buildings is not difficult. Use the pastel lightly so that the paper pattern shows through; it seems, somehow, to look like the bumpy surface of old stone or concrete.

See how little it takes: just two houses in any kind of detail and a church in the background, and your eye fills the entire landscape with a city!

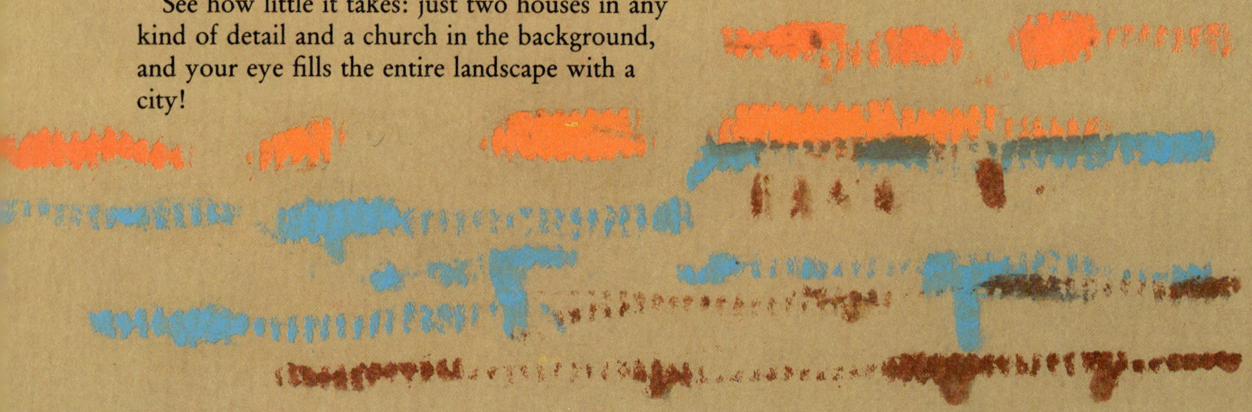

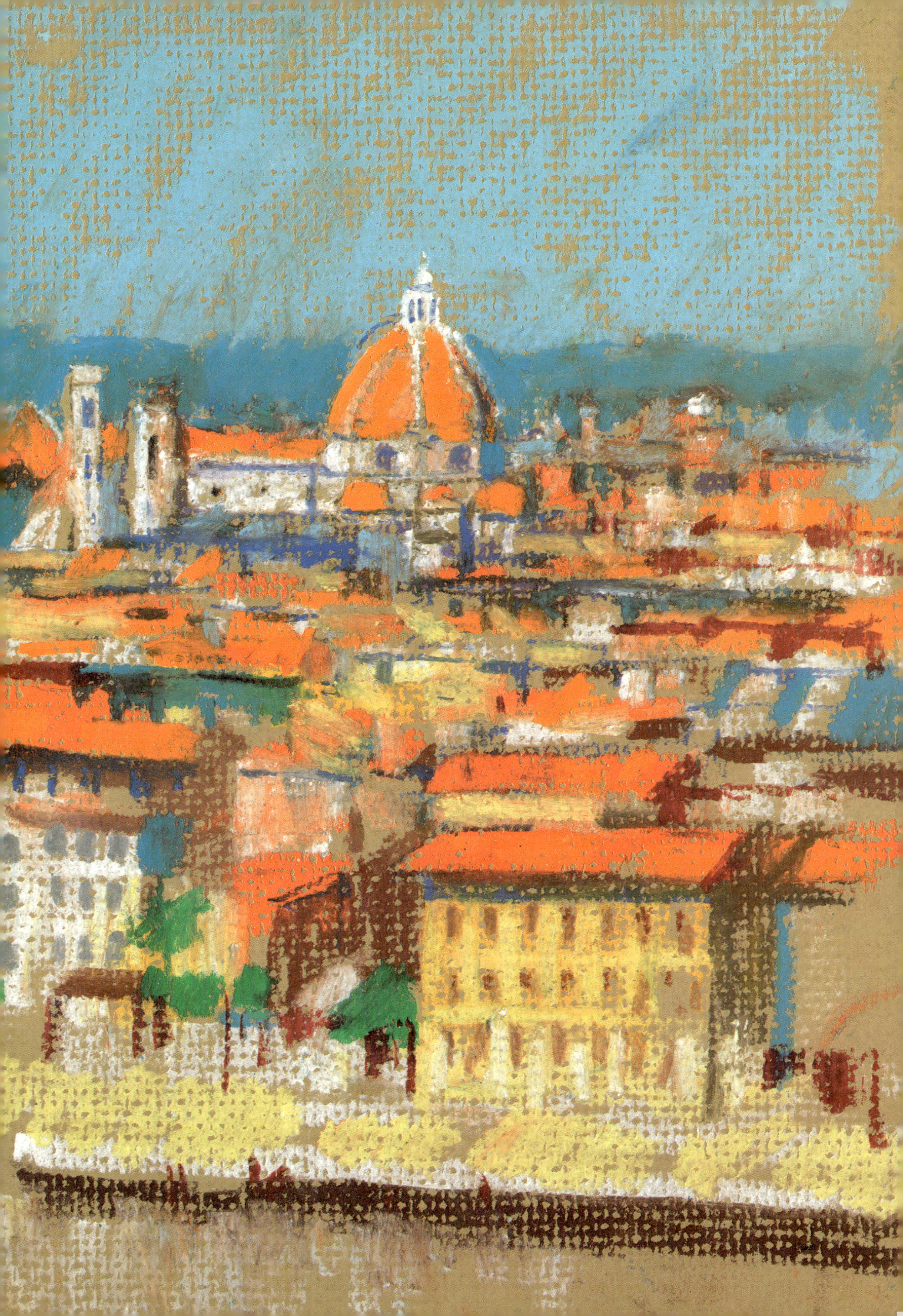

Project 21 Making a Background

Beads

The beads lay on an antique market stall, glittering in different colours, shapes and sizes. I could visualize them on a background of grey velvet, emphasizing their decorative value.

Pastels are a marvellous tool for impromptu drawing. Having a pad of white paper with me and a box of pastels with some fixative, it was too good an opportunity to miss.

When you don't have a suitable tinted background, create your own. Choose a reasonably large stick, lay it on its side, and with long side-strokes cover the entire surface, lifting off as seldom as possible.

In order to give the background a blended texture, 'wash' over the paper very lightly with a damp rag or sponge, so that the tint smudges. Then lift the paper away from you and blow off the surface dust. Fix the pastel colour thoroughly and let the paper dry.

Practise making your own backgrounds at home, until you are confident of the amount of colour needed to make an even surface.

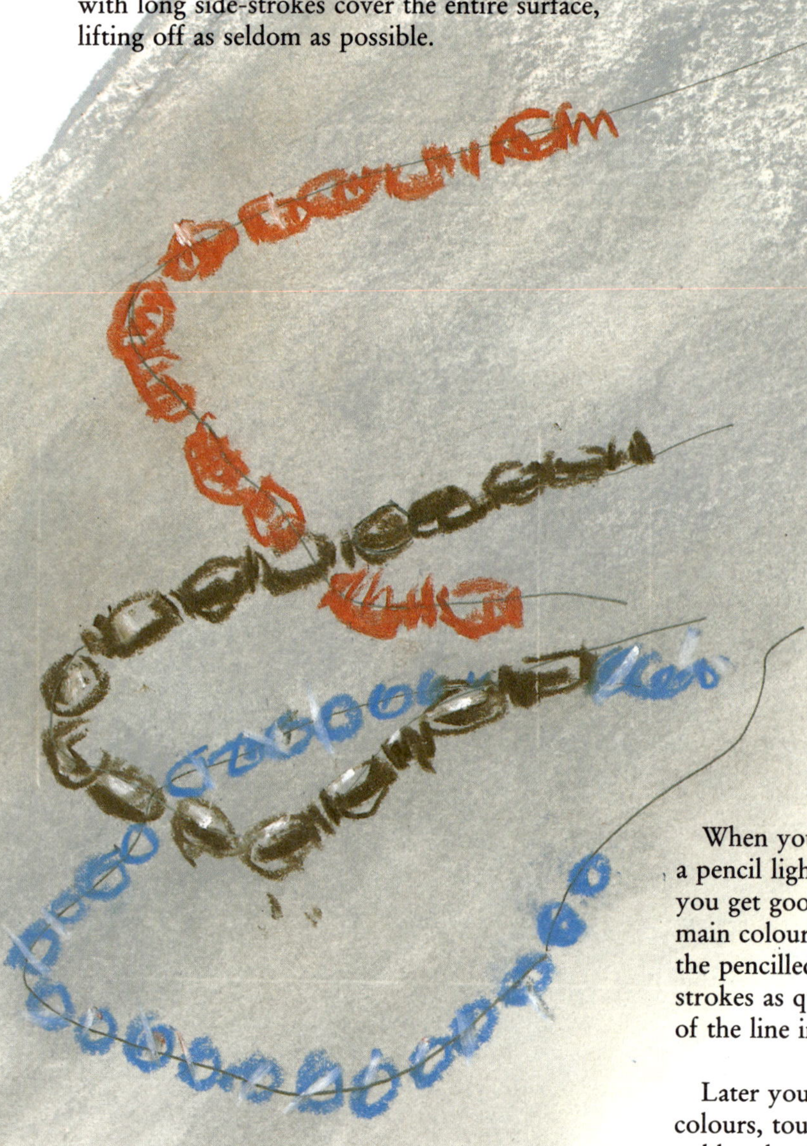

When you are ready to add the beads, sweep a pencil lightly in loops over the sheet, so that you get good, natural curves. Then take the main colour of each string and work down the pencilled line, making short, fairly heavy strokes as quickly as you can, to keep the flow of the line intact.

Later you can fill in the details with extra colours, touches of white highlights, glints of gold and red, and so on. But the secret of this project is to work quickly so that you don't lose the natural fall of the linked chains.

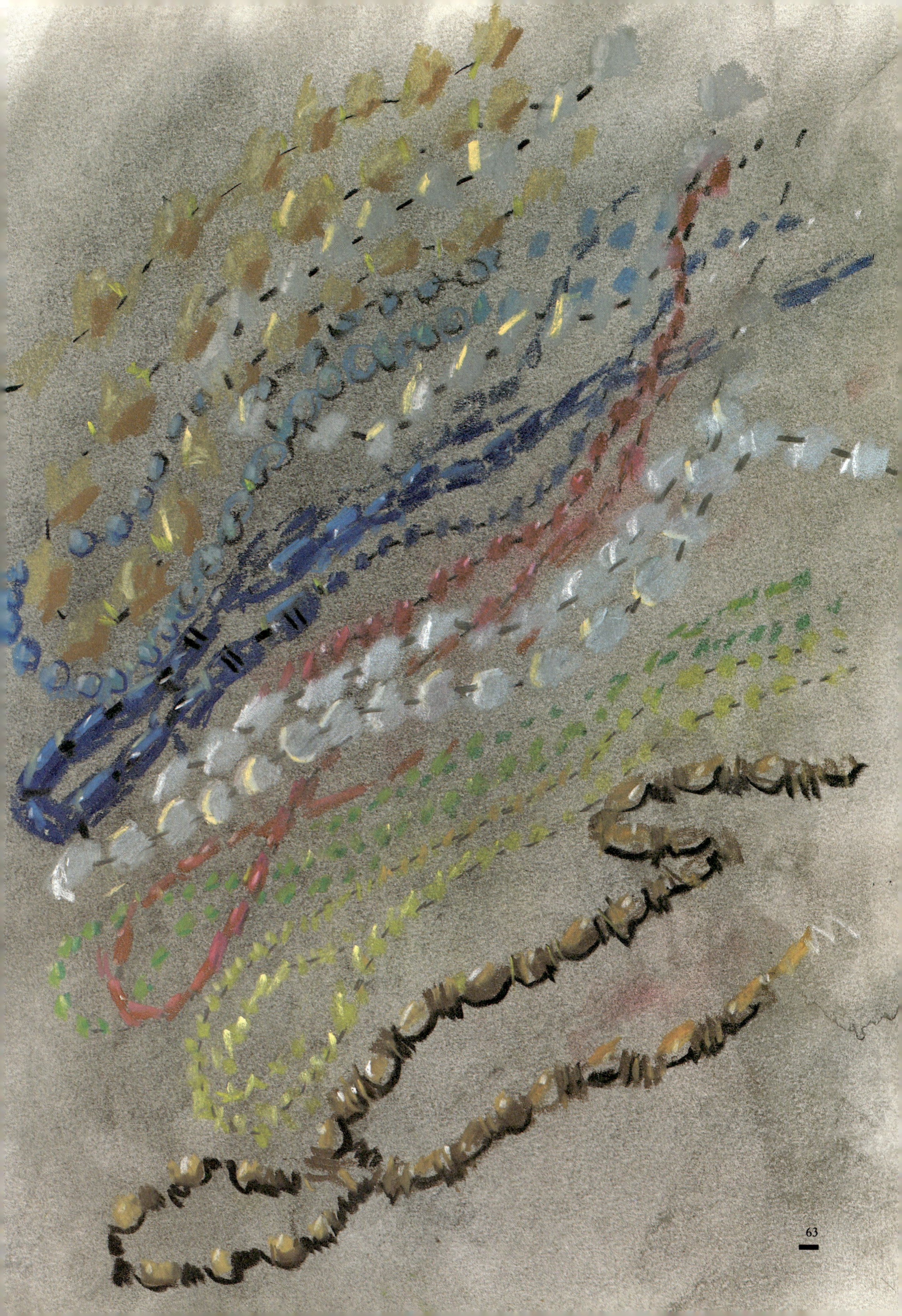

PART EIGHT: UNUSUAL TECHNIQUES

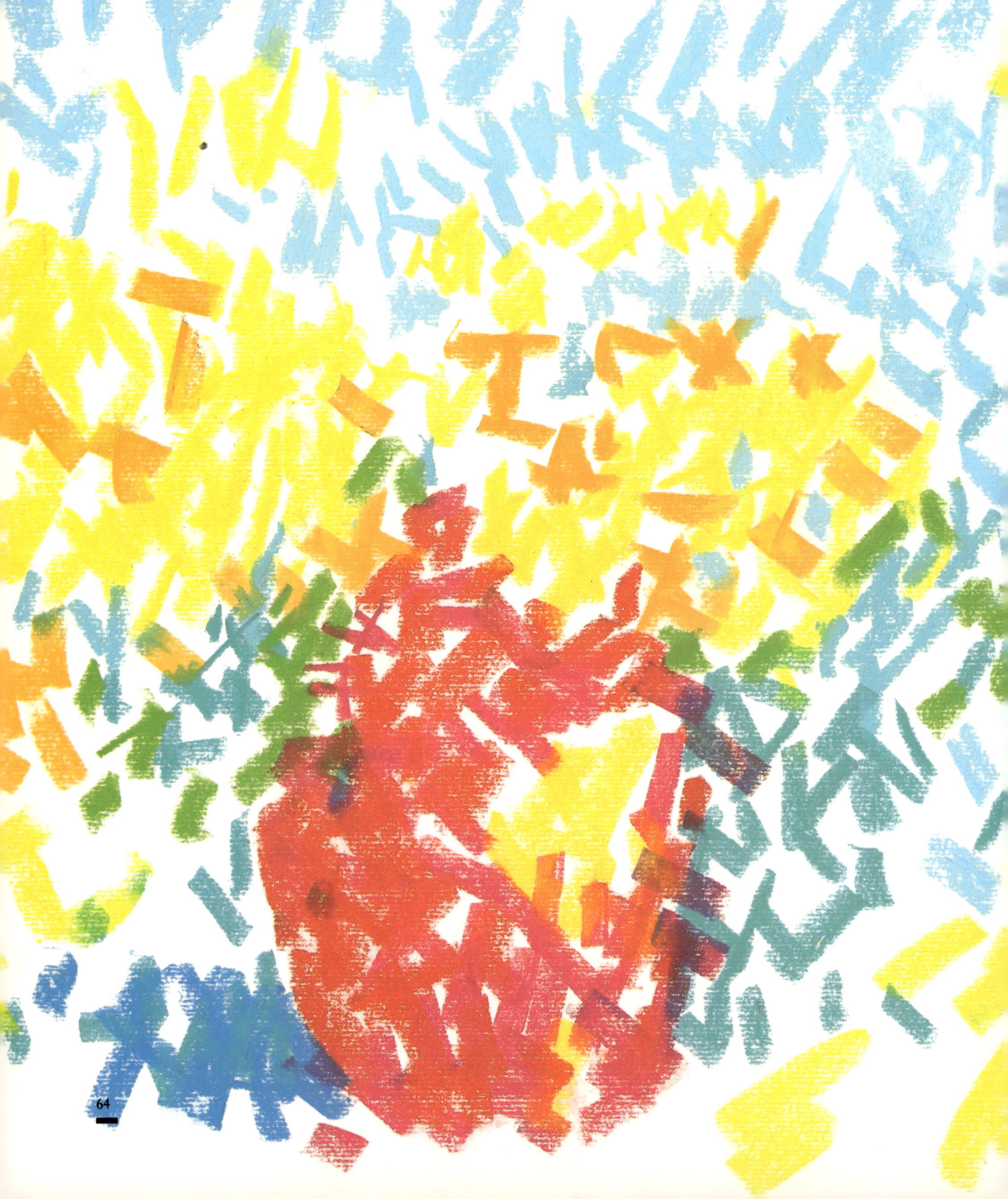

Pastels are so exciting these days that it is difficult to stop thinking of new and wonderful things to do with them. I've tried to pin down some of the possibilities so that you can see how much can be done with only a few resources.

Negative imaging is a very old idea that has become extremely popular since the advent of photography and, now, of holography. It is based on looking at the edges that define the space around the object, rather than at the object itself. It is a wonderful tool for fooling the mind into seeing what isn't there. Drinking glasses are particularly adaptable to this technique, as they often look as if they aren't there either.

'Isms' have become one of the bugbears of the twentieth century. Once used mainly of theories and political beliefs, the word ending has been tacked on to so many ideas that almost every artist can now claim to have invented an 'ism' of his or her own. None the less, the Impressionists have left us with one important 'ism', pointillism, which most of us enjoy because the theory actually creates the art rather than the other way round.

Finally, with the growing popularity of oil pastels, we have the opportunity to use some of the old oil techniques in a new way: scratching, or sgraffito, has been a technique used on pottery and in painting for thousands of years; now we can add oil pastels to the list of suitable mediums.

But don't let your ideas stop there. These projects are intended to be a stepping-stone to new concepts of your own.

Three Glasses

Glass is the best subject for this project, so find three or four wine glasses, crystal cups or vases. Cut-glass helps to catch the light, but most drinking glasses will do. Avoid heavy industrial glass, however, which has little light-catching quality. Even a pair of spectacles will do, as long as you don't start looking for them when you begin to work!

Try to use different shapes and sizes. The idea is to draw around the shapes that the glass makes, not to draw the glass itself. You are looking for the reflected light on the rim and base, the softer reflection from engraving, the sharper sparkle where a beam hits a cut stem.

The colour of the glass does not matter, as long as it is transparent. But clear glass is the easiest to begin with, and opaque glass of any kind is very difficult.

If you are not sure of the concept, then replace the glasses with anything that is matt-surfaced; you will see immediately that it has no shine or sparkle to set off its shape.

It is a good idea to turn down the main light, and work with just one source of light coming from the side. Then half-close your eyes as you look at the models, and draw just those sparks of white where you see the glitter or reflection.

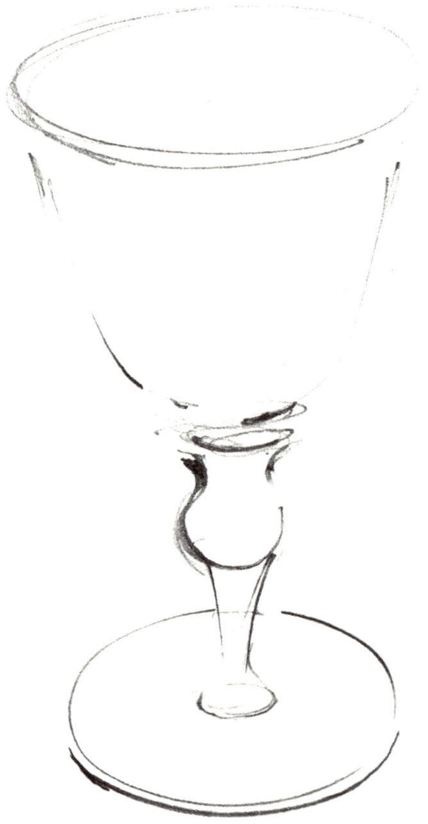

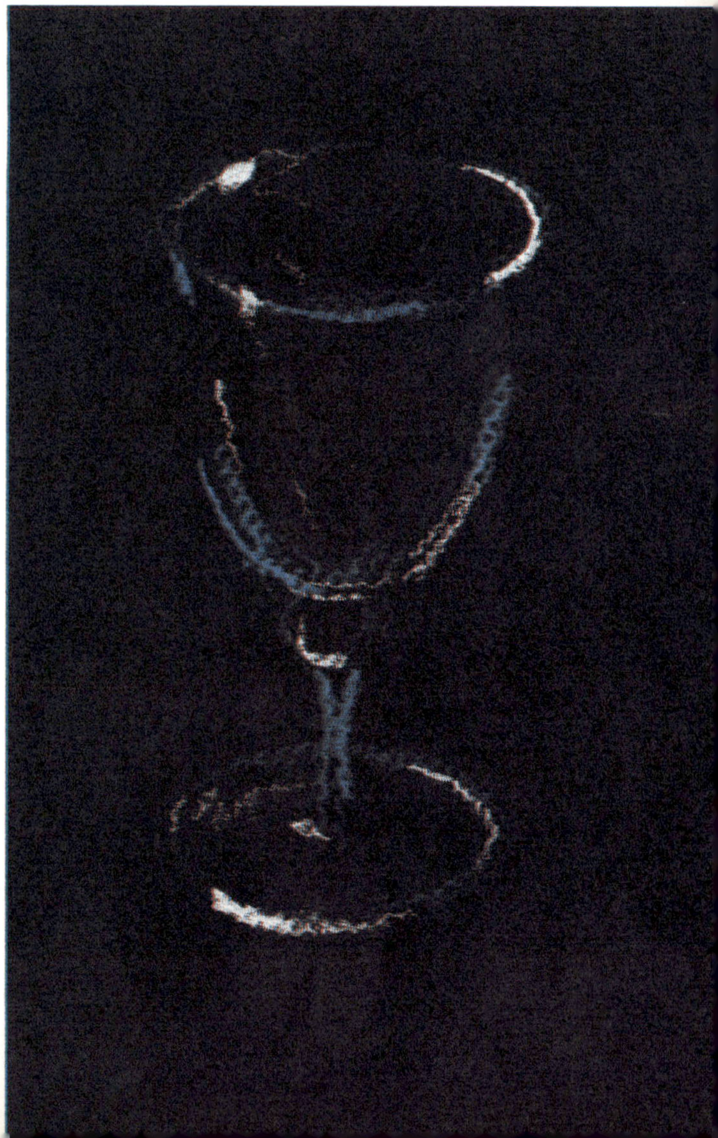

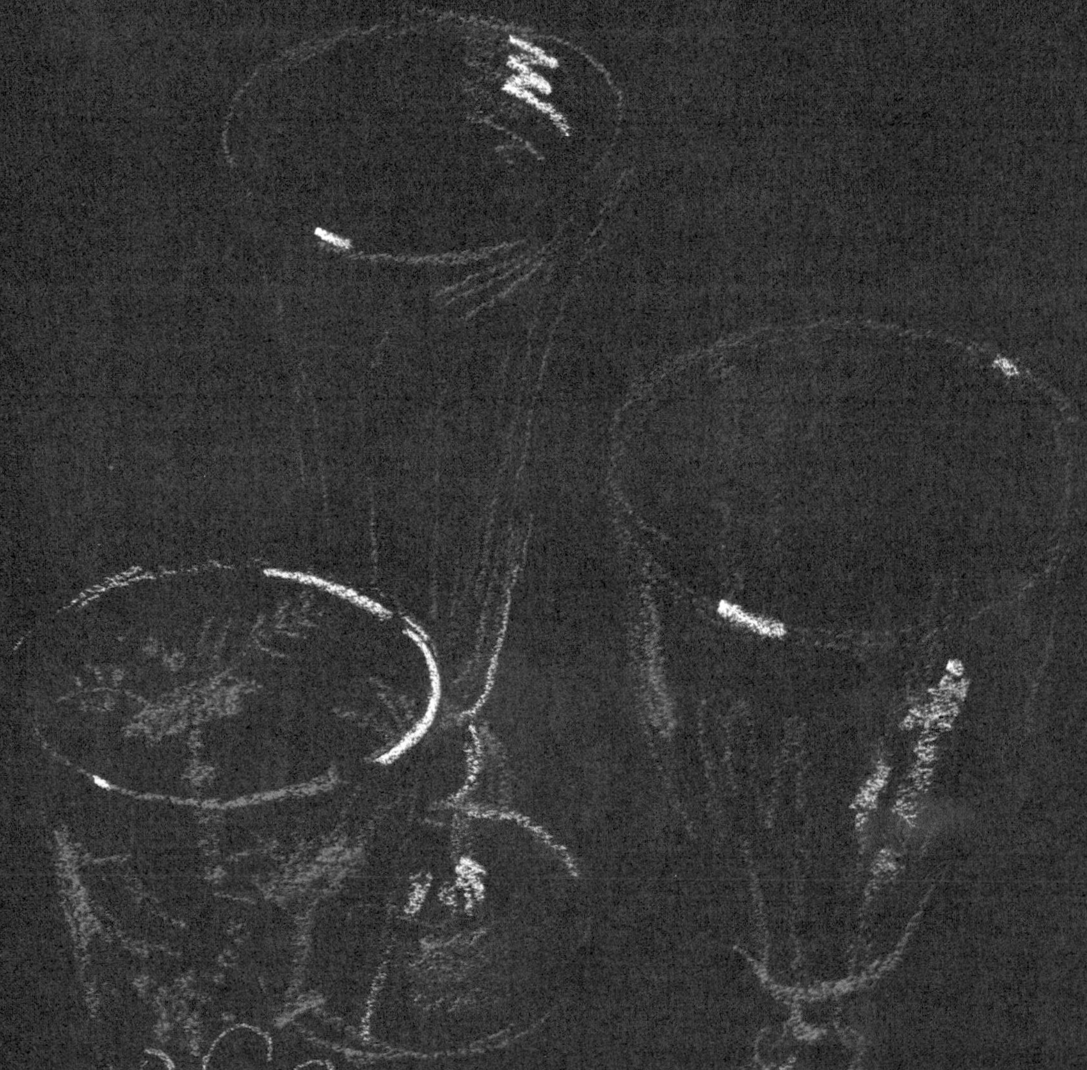

Low Tide

Of all the modern theories about art and vision, perhaps only a few have become part of our everyday vocabulary. Pointillism grew from the nineteenth-century fascination with science, and it attempted to create a revolution in the way we see the world around us. It was based on a theory that is no longer accepted – our optical nerves do not register dots of colour in the way suggested by the earlier scientists – but the explosion of paintings by Seurat and Signac turned the theory into a style that continues to be attractive and useful to the artist.

Pastels are superbly suited to the pointillist technique: separate, small points, or dots, of colour build up the picture. Nothing could be more useful for this than a pastel stick – each little stroke will be the same colour and of the same intensity.

To try out the style, set yourself a subject with plenty of light, and with colours that are closely related. A single cube, a vase or a cup and saucer are good models to practise on.

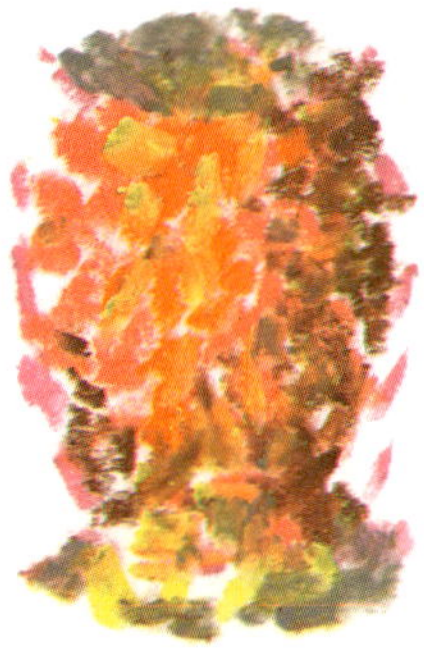

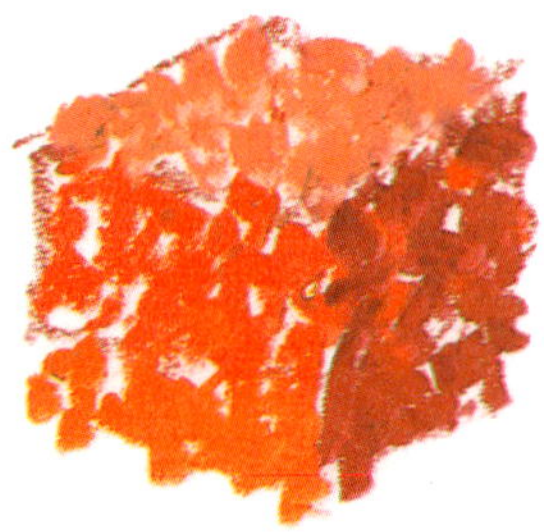

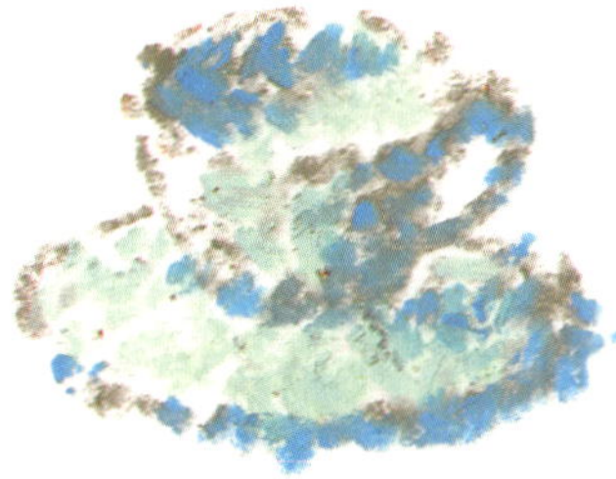

Later, you can look for a wider scene. These boats are just right: strong shapes, bright colours, and a noonday sun creating shadows on the bows. Don't worry about the detail, just block in the shapes with little strokes in the different tones. You can vary the size of the strokes, too.

I let the white paper do its work once again by putting in fewer dots on the left side of the hulls to represent points of light. Perhaps I cheated a little by leaving the sky in one colour, rather than creating modulations with different colours, but I prefer the clear look it gives to the finished sketch.

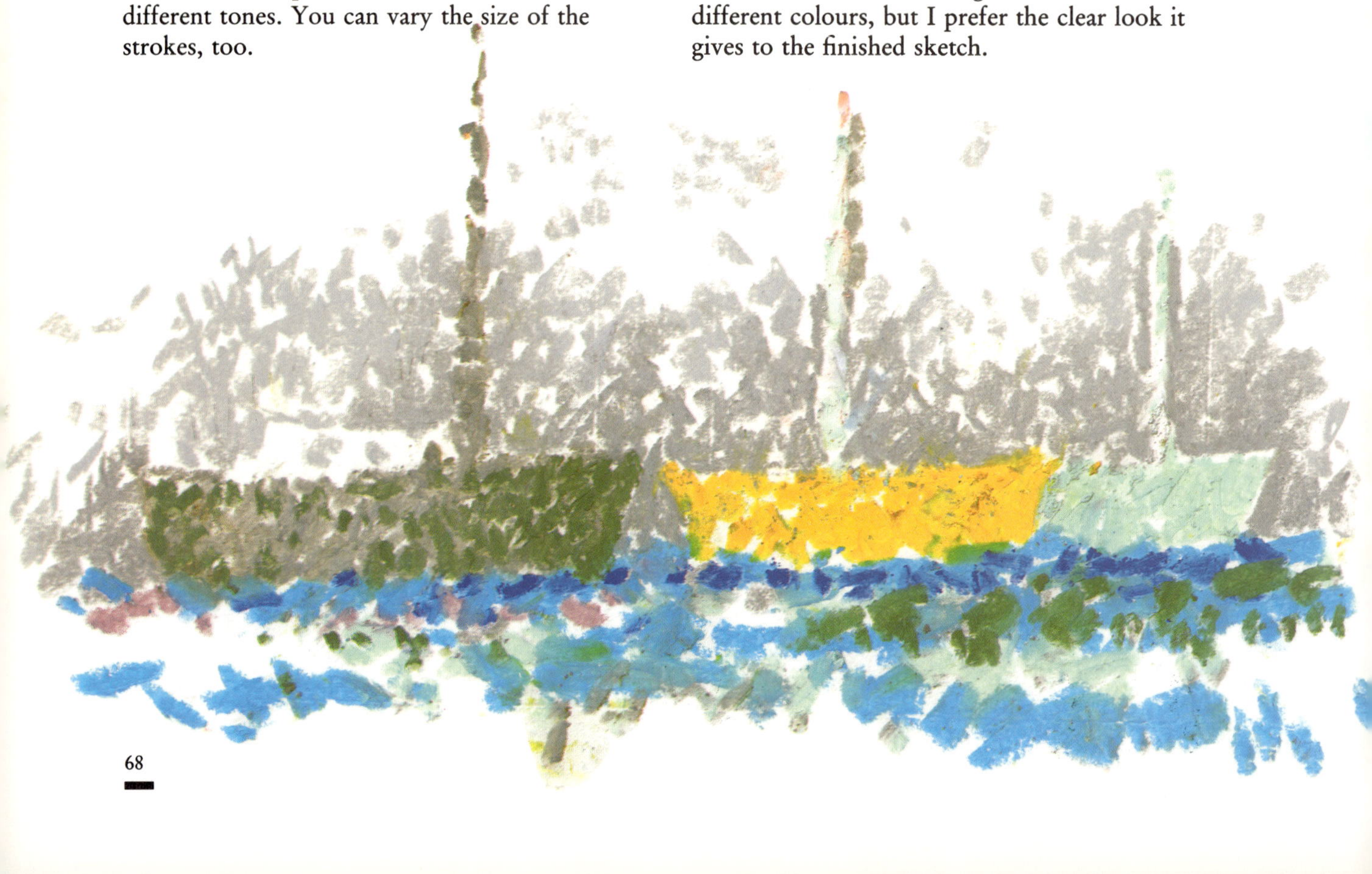

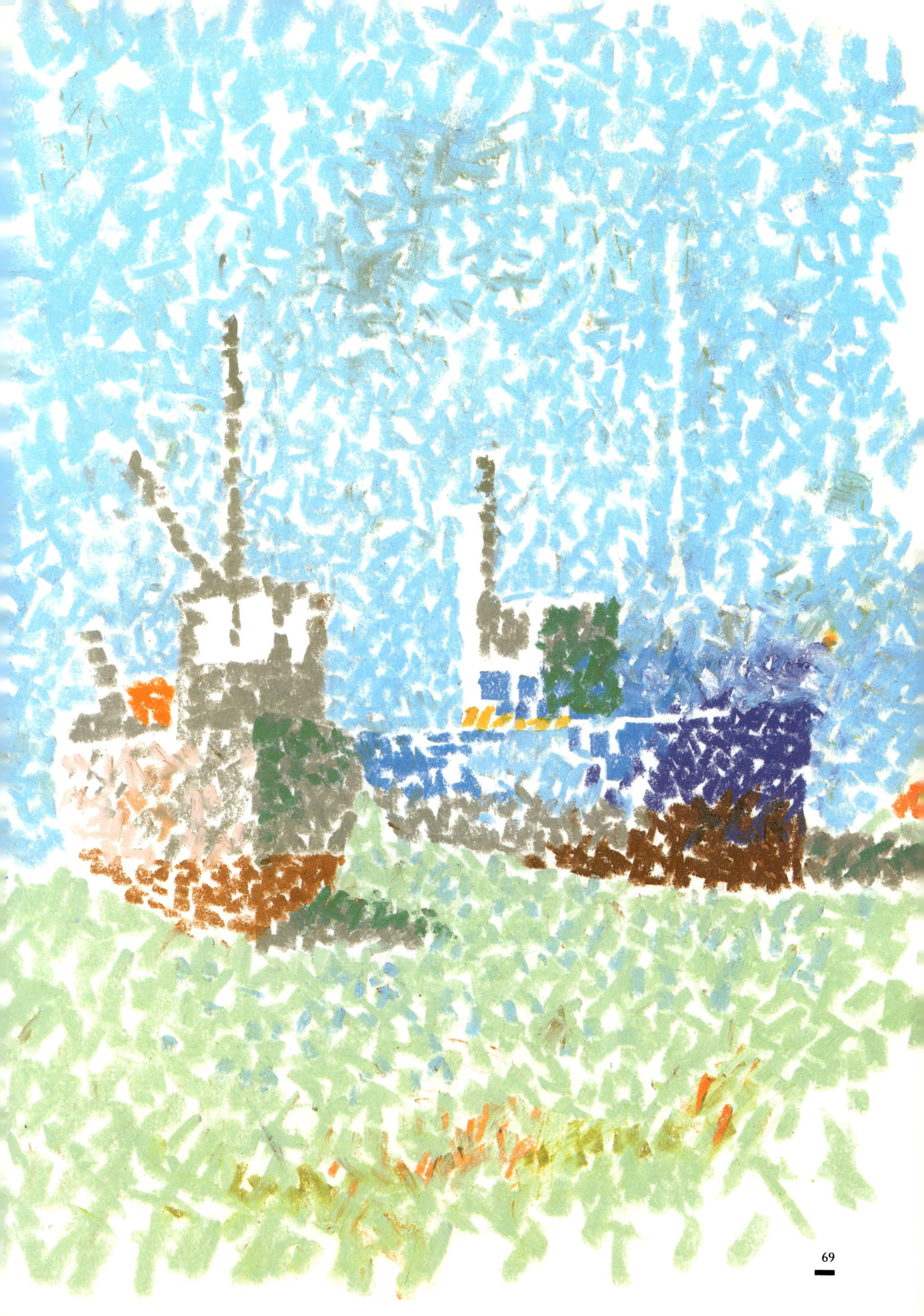

Church Window

Cutting through layers of paint is a technique most often used with oils. However, with oil pastels, which can build up a thick layer on the paper, it works just as well.

There are a few restrictions. Because of the paper base, there is a limit to the depth of pastel you can scrape off without digging into the fibres; in addition, the best effects will be achieved when the thin line of the scratched design contrasts with the heavier pattern of the drawing. This church window sketch fulfils both conditions.

Practise on scrap paper before you begin to sketch, so that you learn to gauge the depth of your surface. Cover the paper completely with heavily worked strokes, then let it dry as much as you can. In humid conditions this can take up to a day or more. You can speed this up with a good fixative, but even so, test the surface with your finger before you continue.

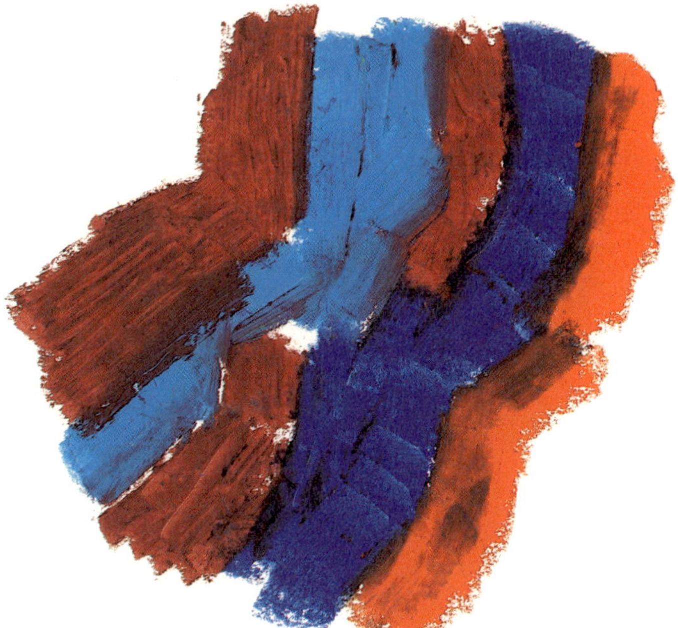

Try out various line designs using the crisp edge of a ruler or a clean, pointed stick. To begin with, avoid using anything that will actually damage the paper, but as you grow more confident you can try a fairly blunt craft-knife. You've got to scratch hard enough to make a clean line through the surface; only practice will give you a feeling for the right pressure.

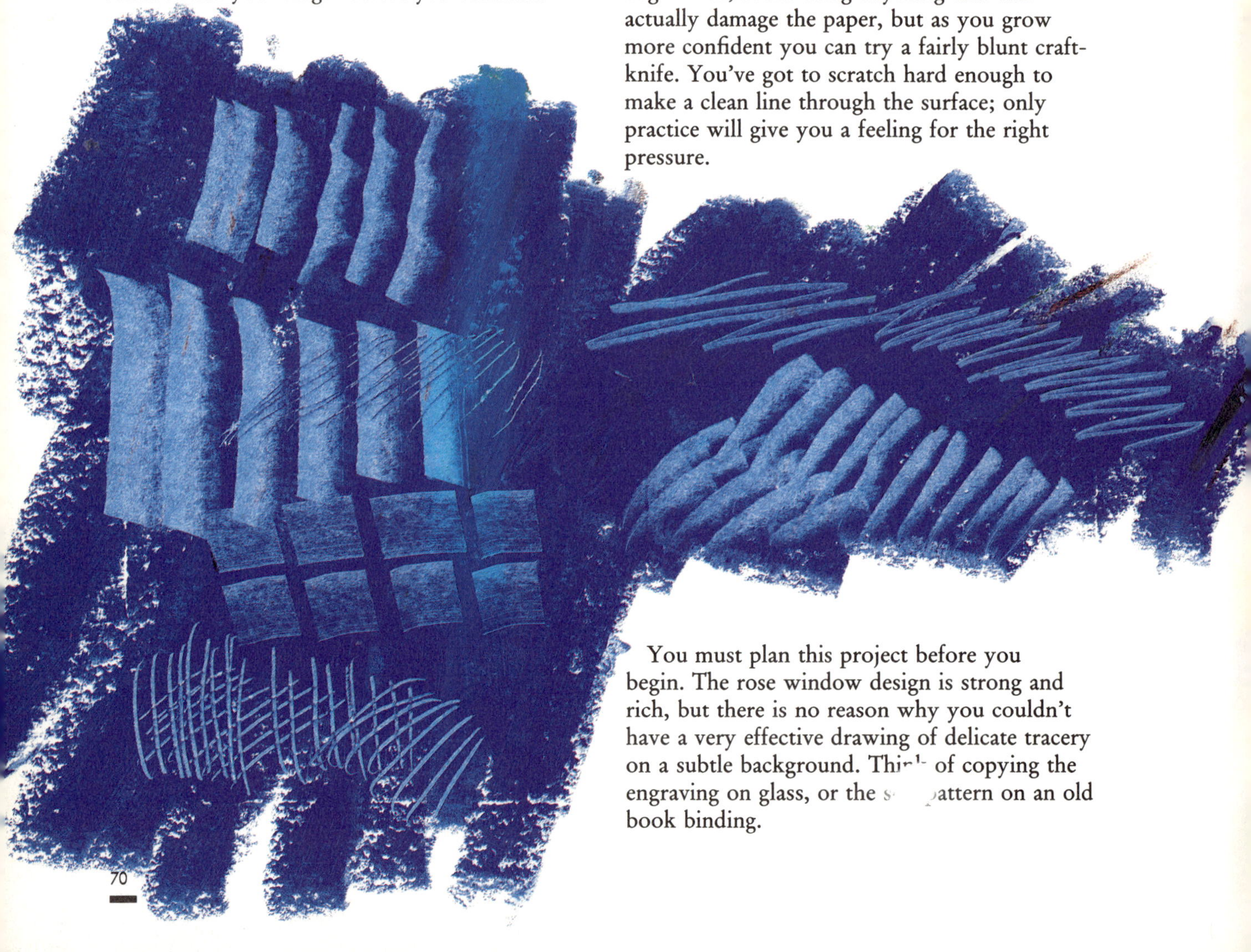

You must plan this project before you begin. The rose window design is strong and rich, but there is no reason why you couldn't have a very effective drawing of delicate tracery on a subtle background. Thi[illegible] of copying the engraving on glass, or the s[illegible]attern on an old book binding.

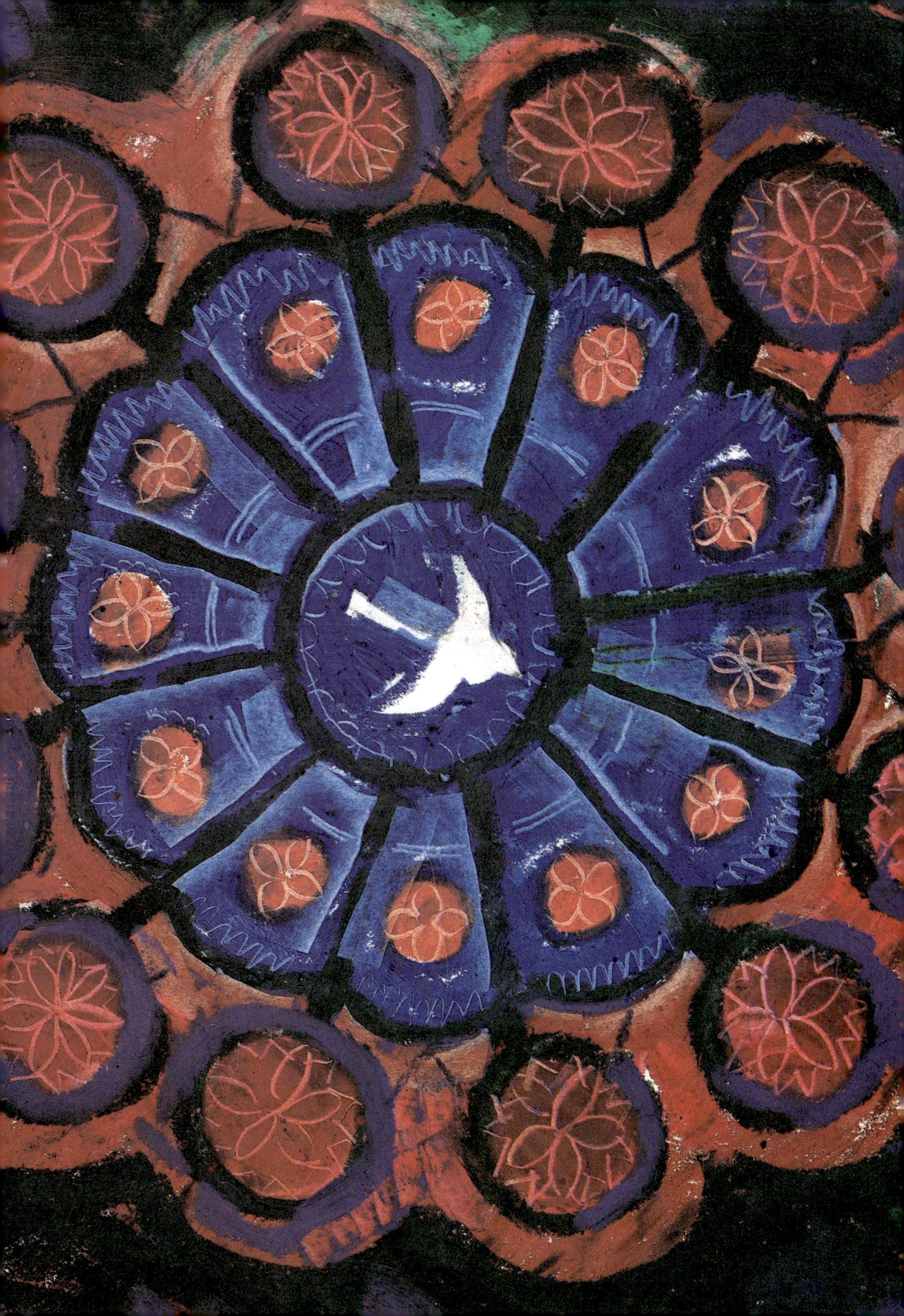

PART NINE: QUICK SKETCHING

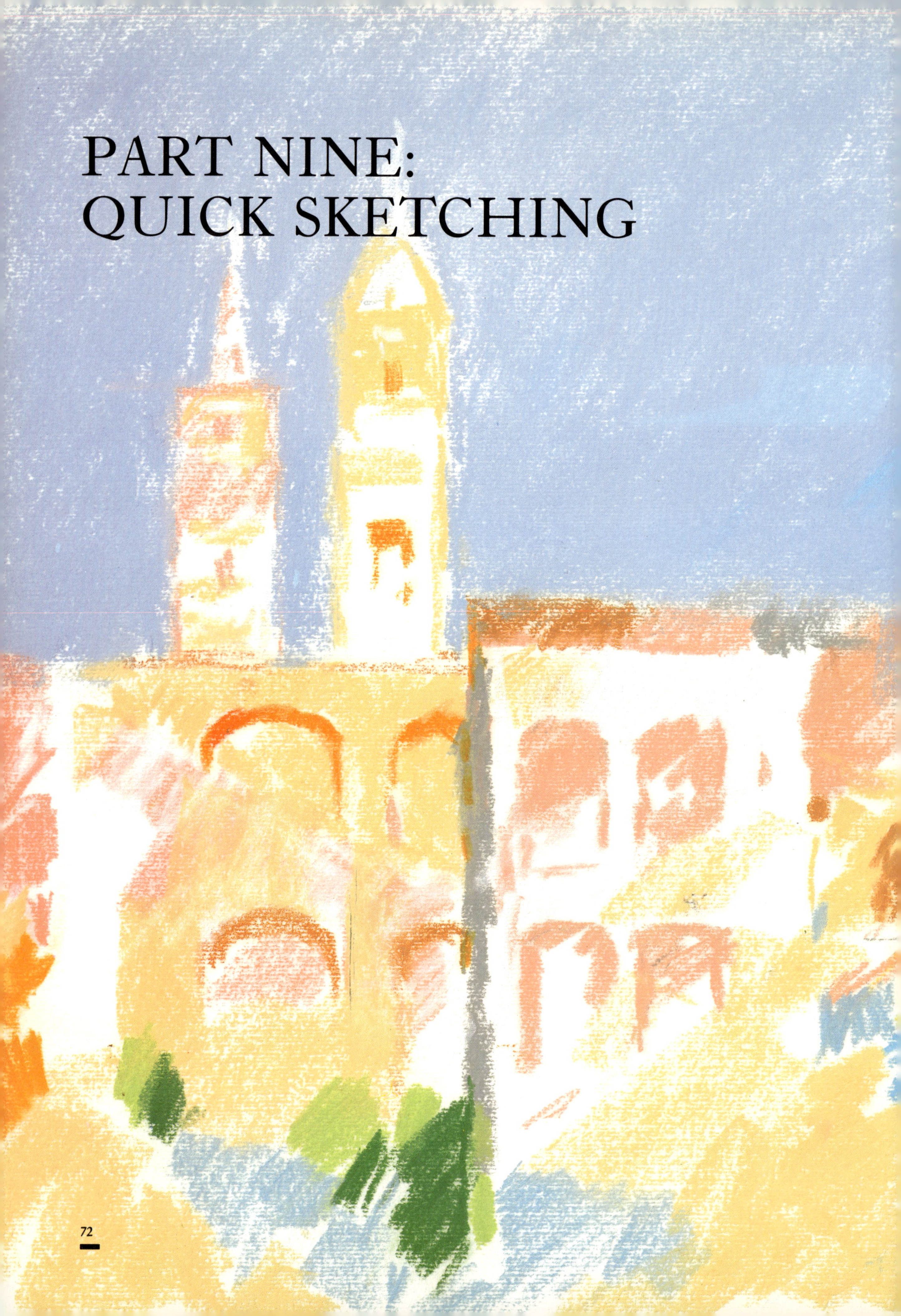

Some of the previous projects have featured sketches that were completed in just a few moments. By now you will be aware how important it is to be able to work quickly when you are outside in the street, on a trip, or making preliminary drawings for a major project.

Because you are working quickly, that doesn't mean that some planning is not necessary. There are useful pocket-sized pads of paper that you can buy, as well as pastel pencils to slip in a pocket; three or four colours would be quite enough for most street sketches. See the Shopping Guide for details.

Choosing the right subject becomes very difficult when there is so much potential everywhere you look.

Learn to select a view or a subject for a particular objective. You may be interested in using strong structural features, so the greenhouse roof of Project 25 could dominate your exterior sketch, just as it dominates the view I saw from inside.

If you were working that day on the control of delicate shapes, then the flowers inside the greenhouse would have been a better choice.

The rather bland street scene of Project 26 is lifted by the red car, just as it would catch your eye in the street; while the figures in the café of Project 27 will help you to catch momentary glimpses of movement and gesture.

Remember to carry a pad, even a tiny one, everywhere you go, and the world will be a place of continuing opportunity.

Project 25 Dominant Features

Greenhouse Roof

This dramatic view of a very ordinary commercial building shows how much fun you can have with common (or garden!) structures. It's all in the way you look at your subject, and being aware of the opportunities around you.

Stressing one feature of any structure will give you variety and surprise – important elements in your work that will keep you keen and alert. In this case I was wandering past some very grey-looking greenhouses near the park, but as I glanced inside the whole scene changed. Light coming down everywhere made the interior as bright as a stage set, the blue sky became deeper, and even the grey industrial rubber flooring reflected the light back.

When such a feature is dominant, make sure you allot it the requisite amount of space on your page. The sketch would have been boring and ordinary if I had focused on the central aisle instead of the roof struts. Look at the sketches below and see the difference for yourself. And I deliberately lightened the colour of the floor, just to let the roof overpower everything.

When working in a hurry, never try to get the detail down. The flowers become blurs of colour, their leaves just scribbles of green. Keep it simple, and concentrate on your chosen feature.

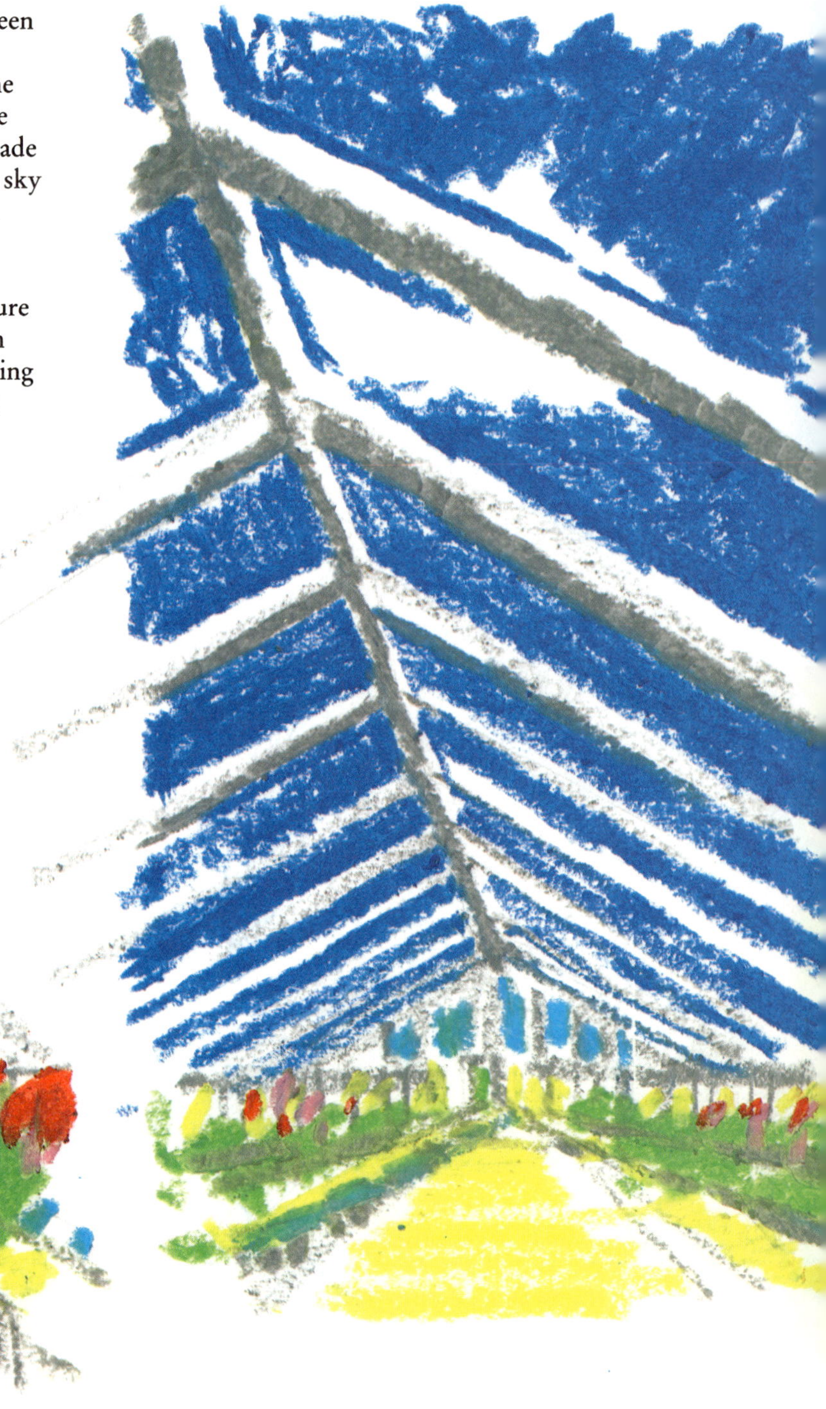

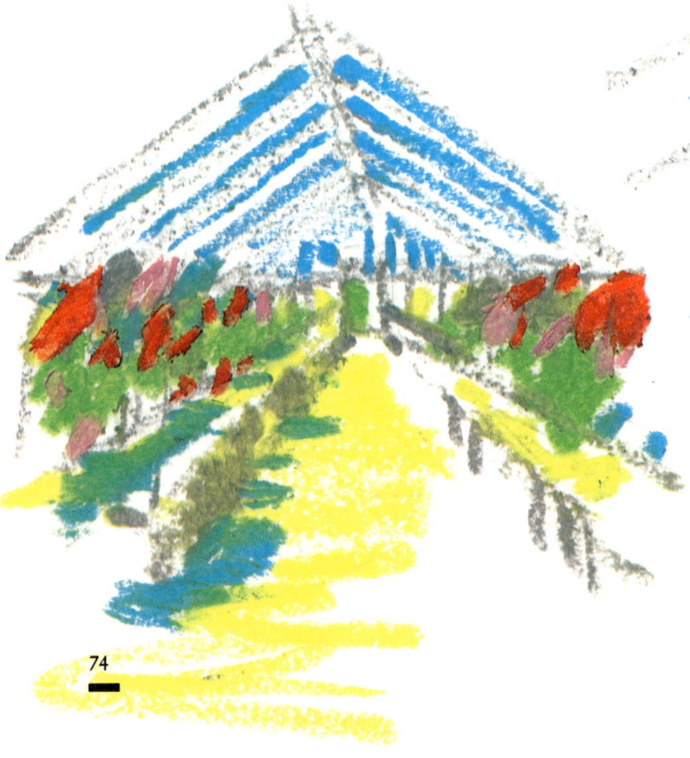

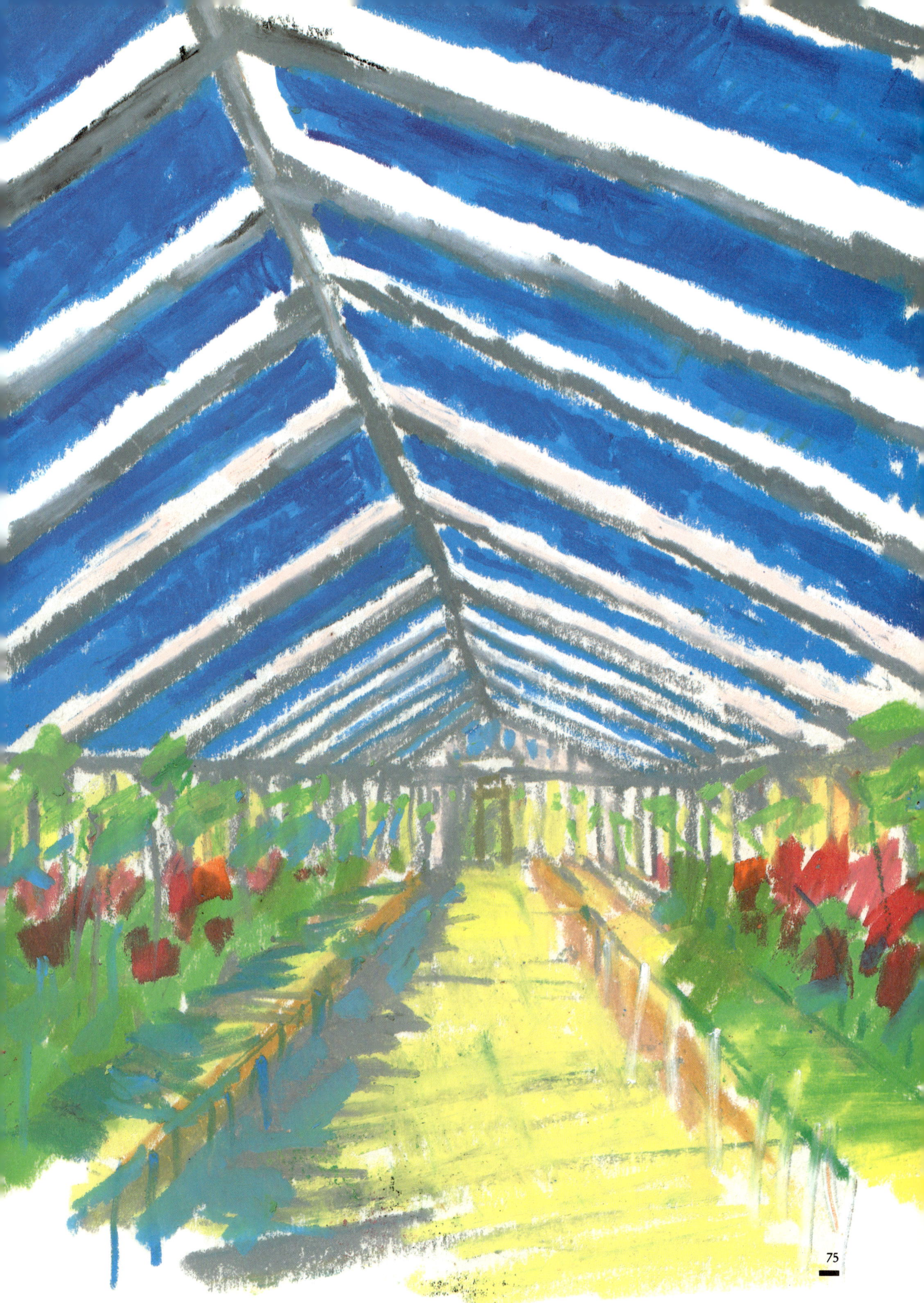

Project 26 Colour Sparks

Street Scene

Most art historians will tell you about the 'spot of red'. In the past, artist after artist wrote solemnly that no matter what the gloom of the landscape or the dark interior of a genre painting, every picture always needed one spot of red to draw the eye.

Well, it is not such a crazy idea, and although I'm not at all sure about 'always' or 'every', there is no doubt that a single focus of bright colour (and it needn't be red, either) does work wonders in turning a pleasant scene into something fresher and more lively.

Try it for yourself; spend a few moments on a similar scene – the atmosphere of an ordinary suburban street – sketching a view towards a facing building. Assume the colour of the parked car is brown or blue. I think you will see the difference, and you have my permission to use artistic licence and change the car to red, yellow or even pink! The yellow touches on the car also add to the effect, even though they are just three quick strokes. Again, don't try to add details; just the barest outlines, with lots of white paper showing through.

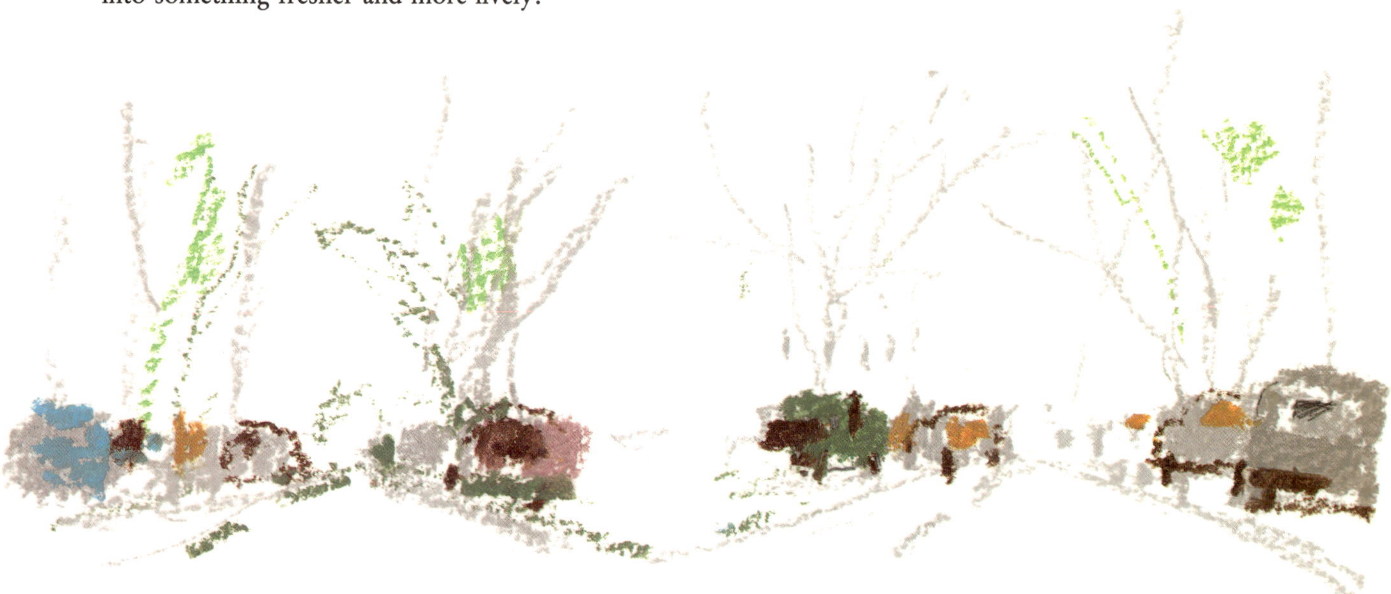

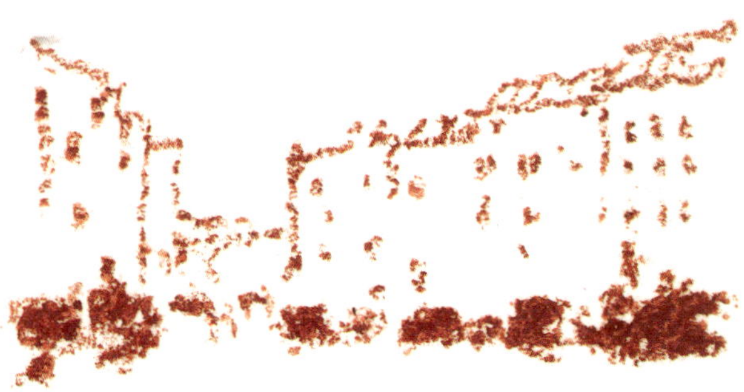

If you haven't thought of including cars in your sketches (perhaps you thought they ruined the view), I hope you will agree that, in this picture, they create an attractive, busy street scene. So try drawing them with minimal lines of black pastel or charcoal, and sketching them from all directions – from the back, sideways, down the street, parked on the kerb, or moving past you.

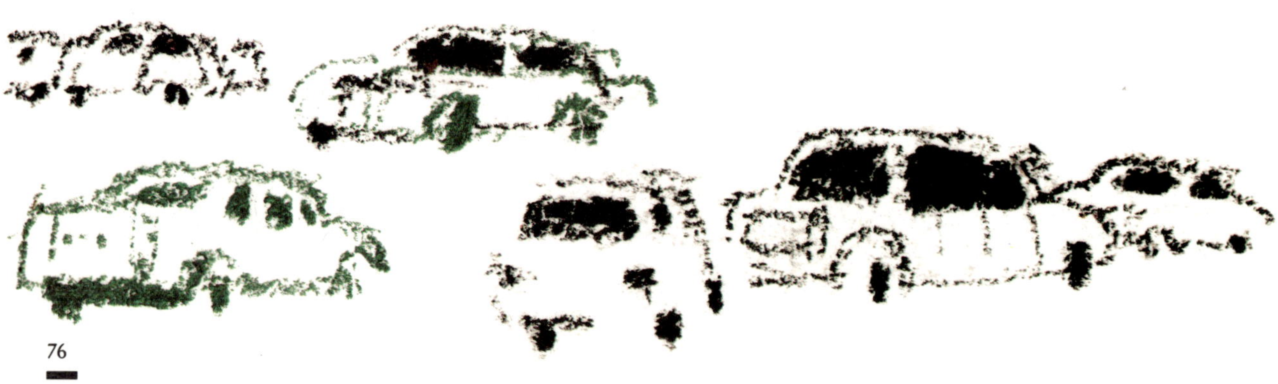

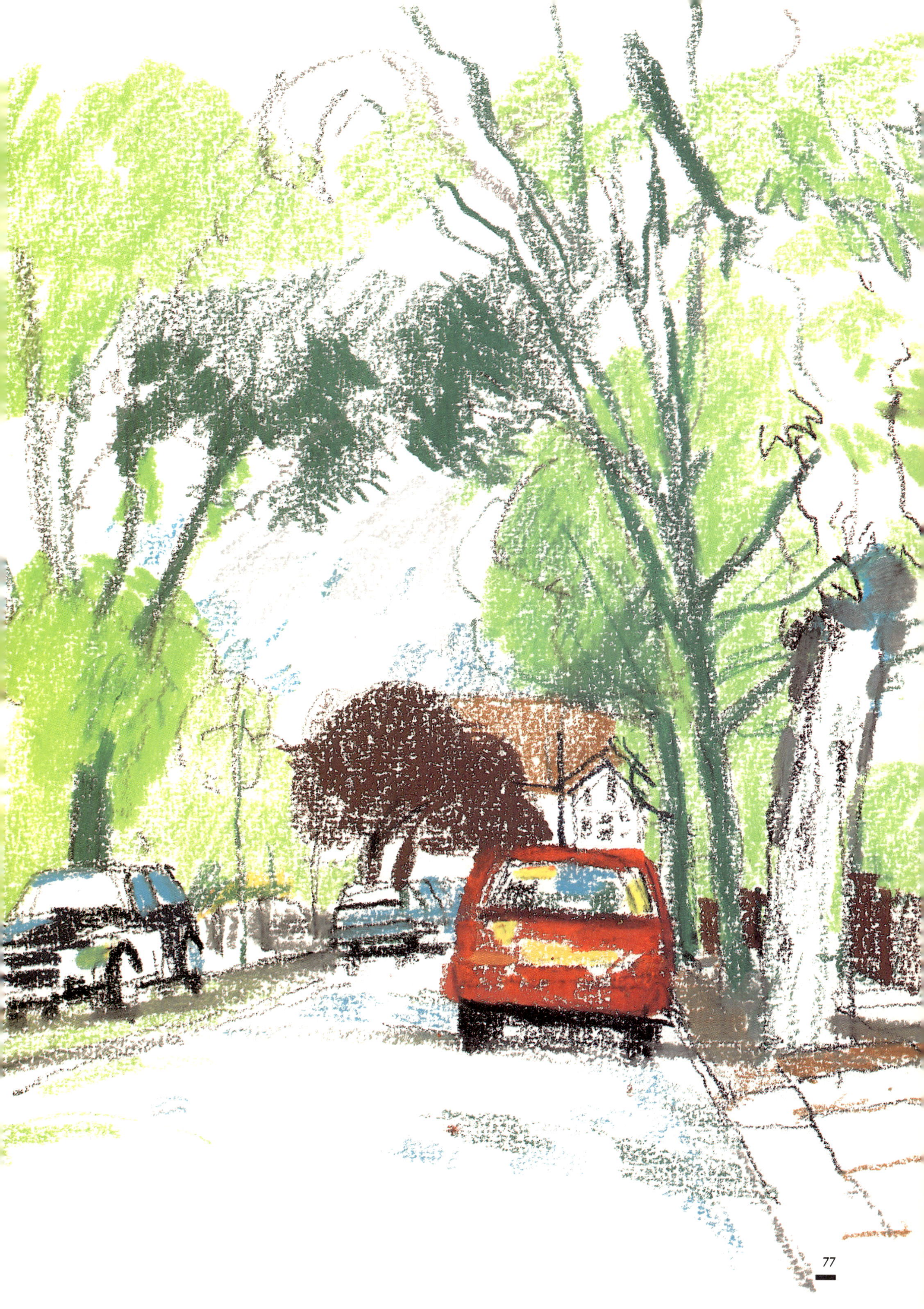

Café Terrace

Many sketches could include people; they add enormously to the lively effect of the composition and give a sense of scale and movement to the lightest drawing.

In the beach scene of Project 19 there were some figures, also quickly drawn and characterized by just a flash of skin and hair. But you will need more than that for your close-up pictures, so start practising by drawing at a restaurant or café. Now that we have all taken to sitting outside in the summer, it is the perfect opportunity.

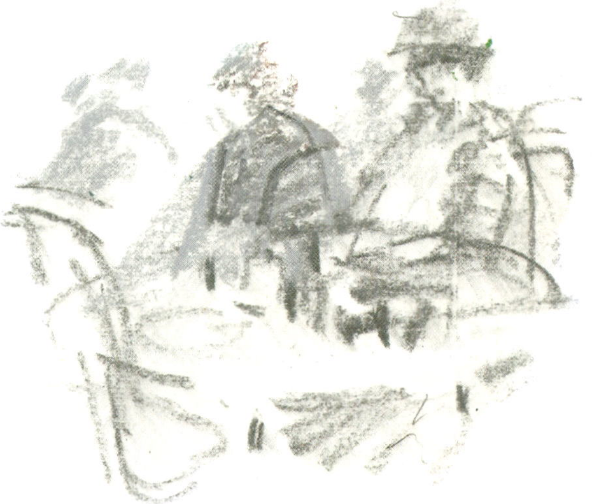

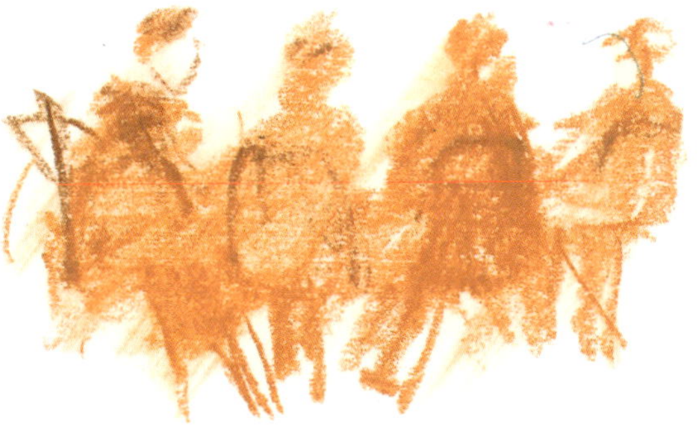

One of the good points about working from a table is that you are relatively unobtrusive. And when you first begin sketching it's a help when people sit still for more than a moment.

Look for the main bulk of their torsos. Scribble in the body and the line of their arms before you add the head. Pastels are good for this, because you can use the broad end of the stick and cover the entire figure in a few seconds.

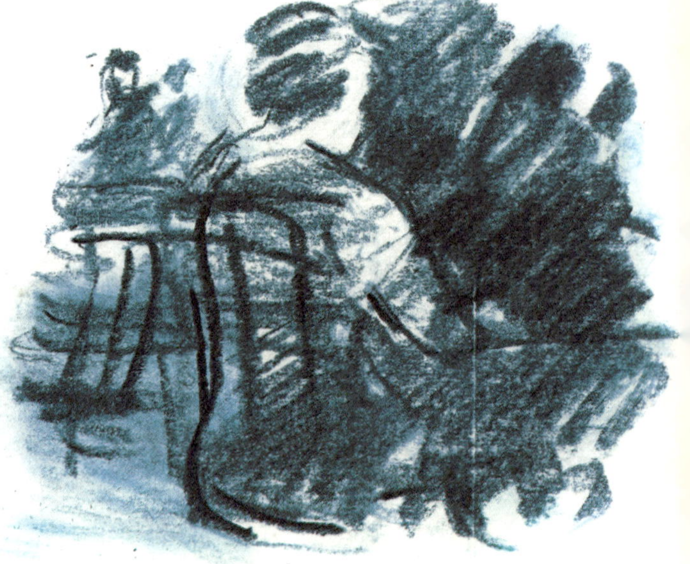

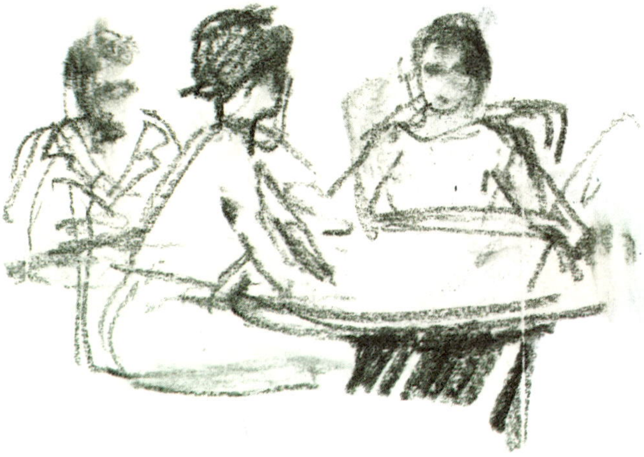

Try to imagine their bulk on the chairs, so that they really appear to be sitting down. Because I was travelling light, I had only a few colours with me, but that was enough. The windows and arches were added when I got home, but they are not really necessary.

Keep sketching people as often as you can: in the street, in the park, even in the train. Work from behind them so that they don't become self-conscious. It is amazing how their uneasy stiffness can communicate itself to you, and to your drawing.

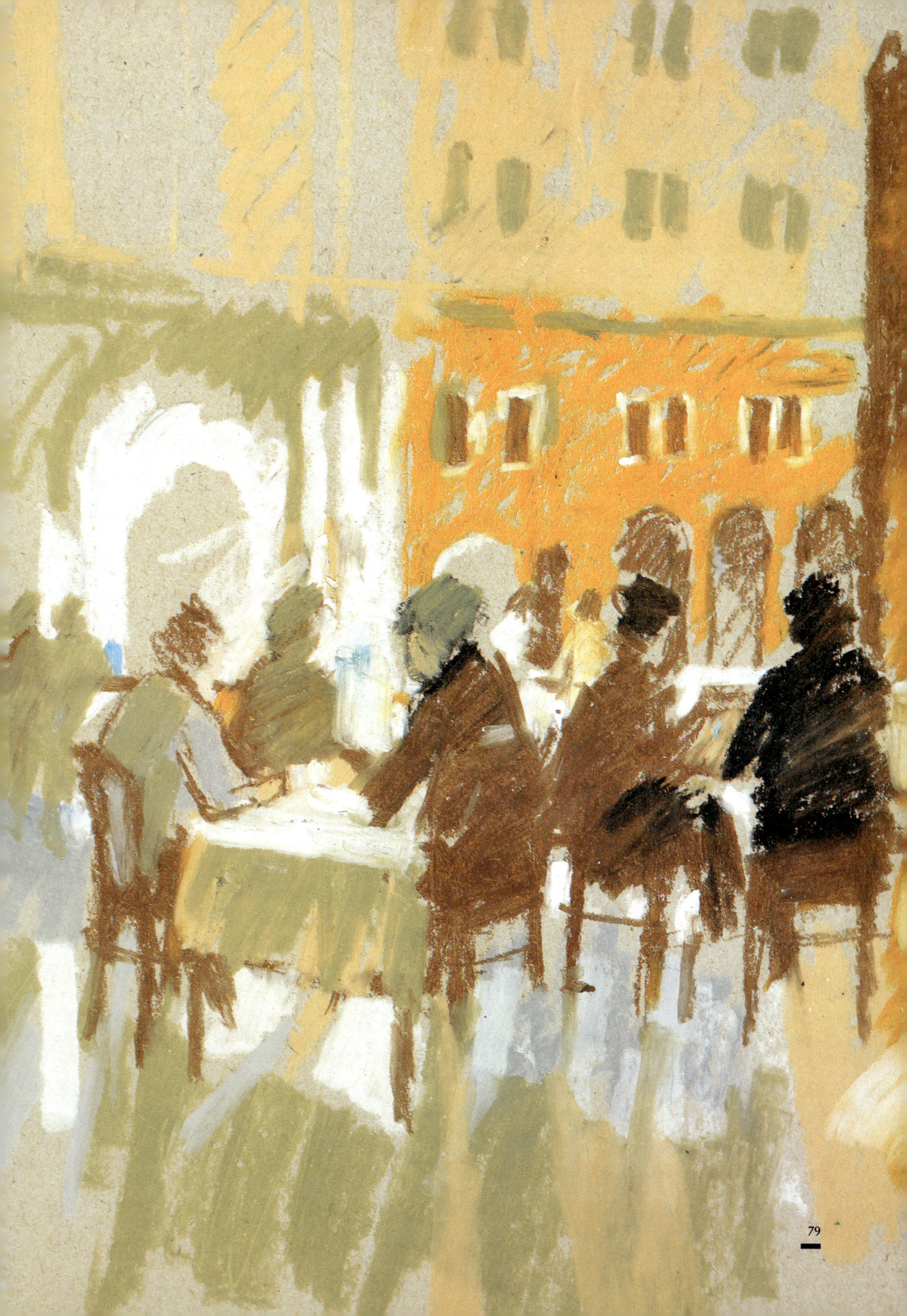

PART TEN: COMPOSITION

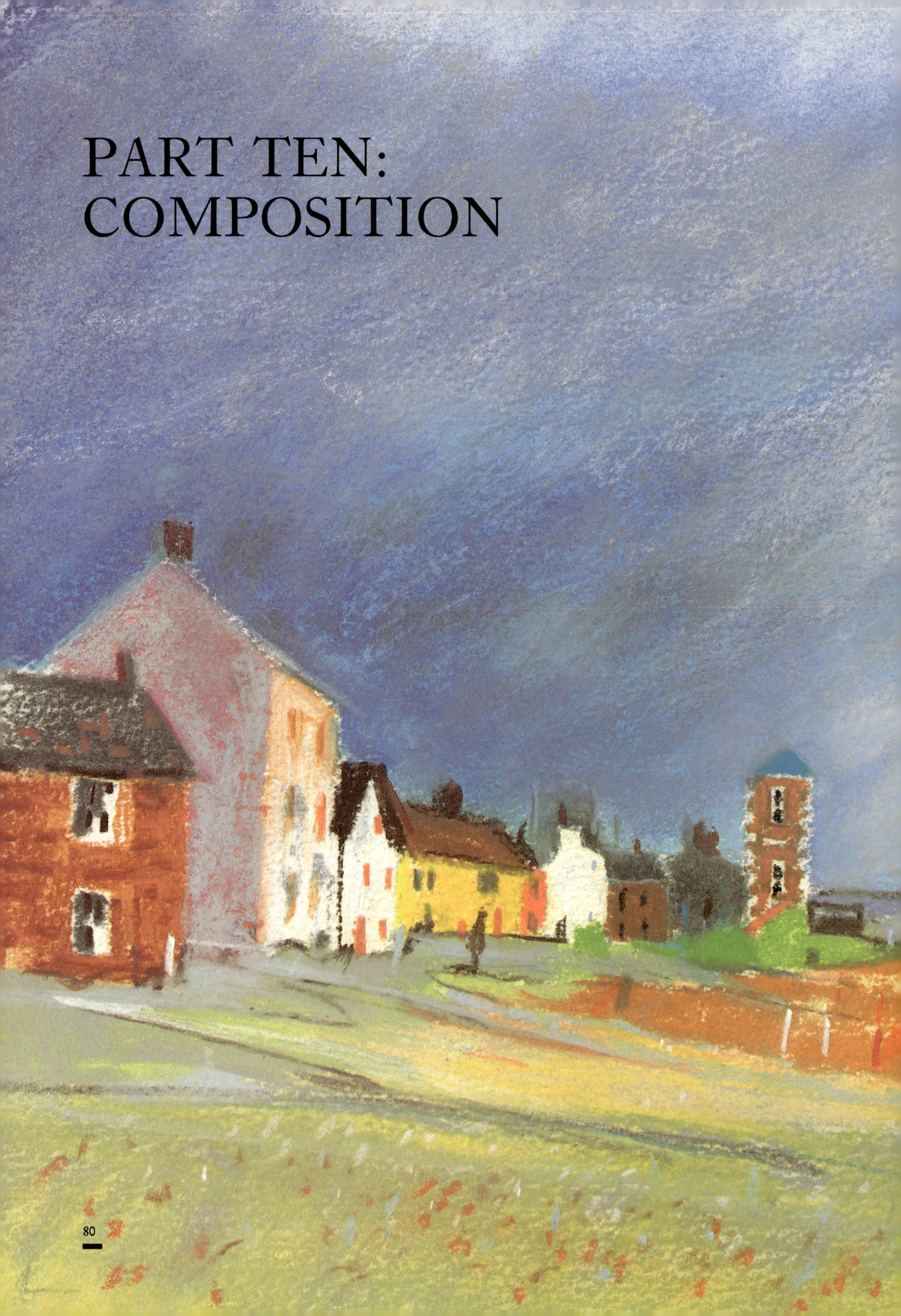

Throughout the many projects and ideas in this book, we've looked at a variety of pastel materials and all the basic techniques that you need to draw successful pictures. Now it's time to put those skills to use in a few more complete projects.

Composition is perhaps the single most important element in good picture-making. But it is also a skill that can be learned, and its basis is much simpler than you might think.

It's as simple as a game of three questions! What do I see? Why does it look that way? What if I changed it?

What do I see? Learn to look carefully at your surroundings. Look at the way sunlight changes a colour. Look at shadows, shapes, sizes, colours, etc.

Why does it look that way? Train yourself to think about relationships: light against dark, sun making shadow, large against small.

What if I changed it? To make an image more interesting, sharper, more exciting? Could I see around the flowers to the window if I moved to the side? If I changed the dull glass for a yellow one, would the rich red look even richer? If the bridge seems too far away, what about a bollard in the foreground?

Learn to play the game all the time – casually while you are working on something else; carefully when you are concentrating on making pictures. There will never be a lack of images to draw, and your work will always – as any good art should – reflect the artist's view of the world.

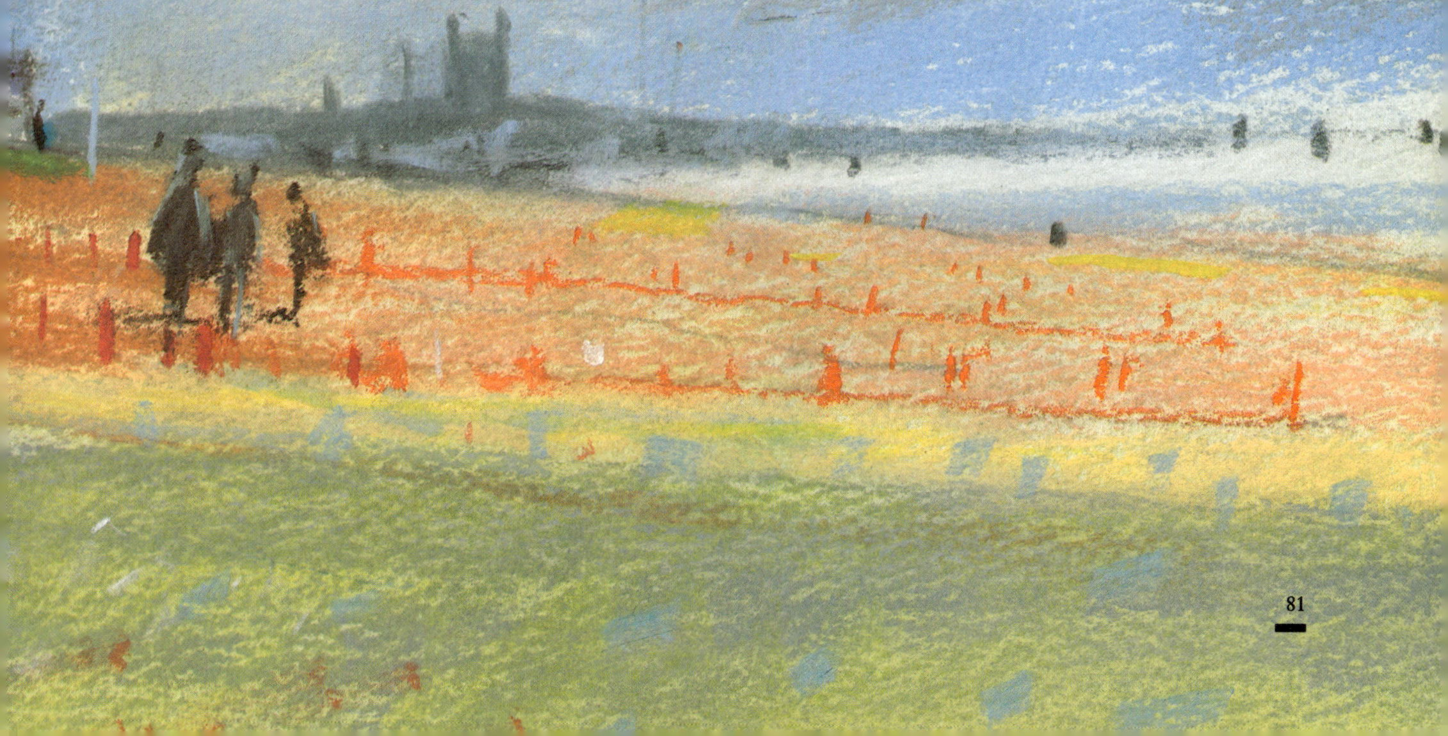

Vase of Flowers

Sometimes you see something so lovely and so striking that you feel it must be right in the middle of your composition! The vase of flowers was just such an inspiration, and I decided to give it centre-stage.

However, I did make a change by sitting down, so that I could draw the flowers fairly low on the paper. Perhaps it is an unconscious result of gravity anchoring us down, or perhaps because we are quite short in relation to our environment, but the fact is that our eyes are more comfortable with the focal point of a picture located below the centre rather than above it. Sketch it that way for yourself and you will see the difference.

Because the picture is full of different images, I sketched it out first in charcoal. That is when I made another change, letting the windows open up at the top instead of closing them off. It brings the eye back to the flowers.

Once the charcoal outline was done, it took very little time to fill in the sketch. I drew the objects first in a few strokes of green and brown, then added the blue background, changing the weight of the pastel to give smoothness and a little more depth where the painted walls frame the flowers. There are just the lightest of blue shadows on the white tablecloth, and a few yellow scribbles beyond the windows.

Finally, three red strokes added a flourish.

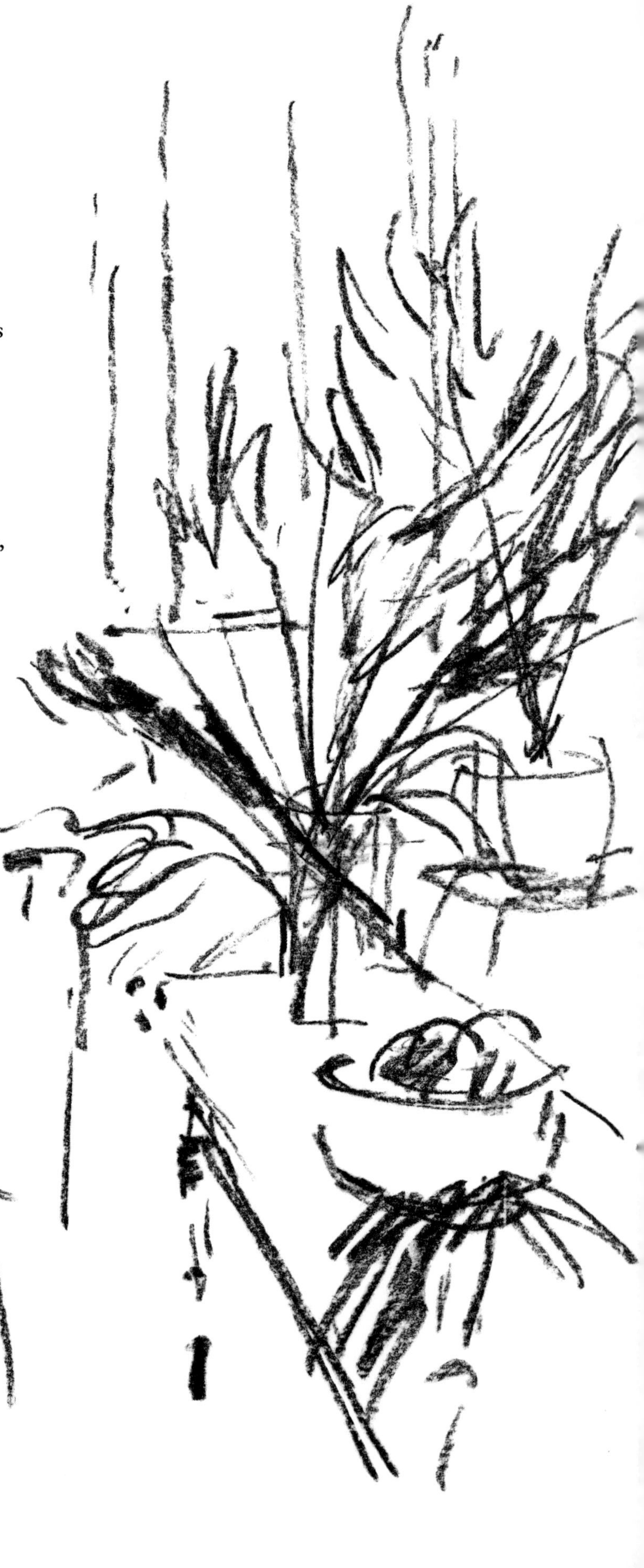

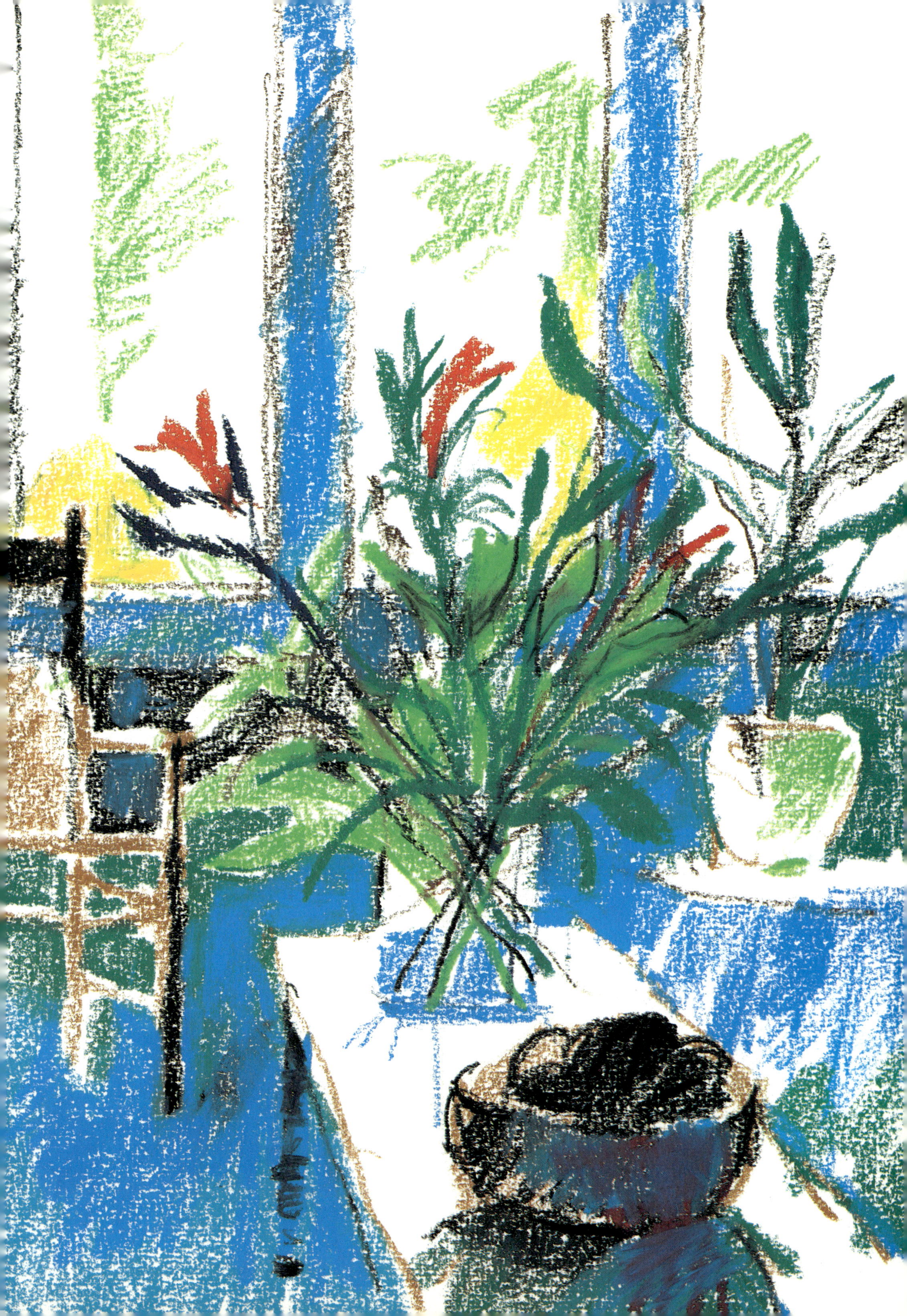

River Scene

Peaceful landscapes have a special appeal in an overcrowded world, and riverscapes offer even more, both to the viewer and the artist. Somehow the reflections in the water do more than double the view; they double the emotional impact as well. So it is not surprising that sketching and painting on the river is one of my favourite occupations.

In this bridge scene I had a few extras that day – a spring-morning sun that softened all the colours, a boat moored just offshore for a spot of extra intensity, and the new fresh green of the trees on the right.

In line with the soft tones, I used mid-grey pastel rather than charcoal to place the image on the paper. The same influence led me to use soft sticks rather than oil pastels. When you make your first placement, remember you can always use colours as well as charcoal.

Pastel is really good for defining quick outlines, because you can choose a very light tone *and* keep the texture light at the same time. There need be only a few flakes of pigment on the paper until you are happy with the result, then you can go over them later with a little more pressure.

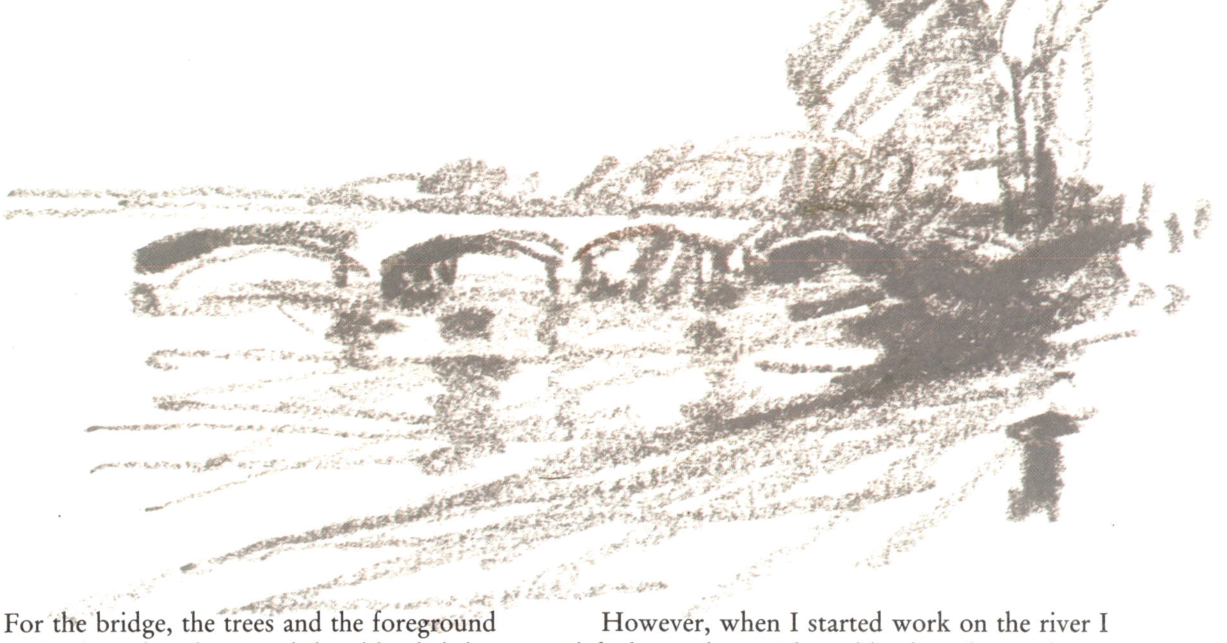

For the bridge, the trees and the foreground I put in the pale colours and then blended them carefully. I had to use the very tip of my finger because the areas were so small and I did not have a cotton-tipped stick with me. The bloom that this technique creates is perfect for the blurred effect of early-morning light.

However, when I started work on the river I left the strokes, without blending them. The open, chalky texture is more appropriate for water. Do remember that reflections tend to shimmer even when the water is quite calm, and the colour changes, too. See the stone pillars turning slightly green under the surface.

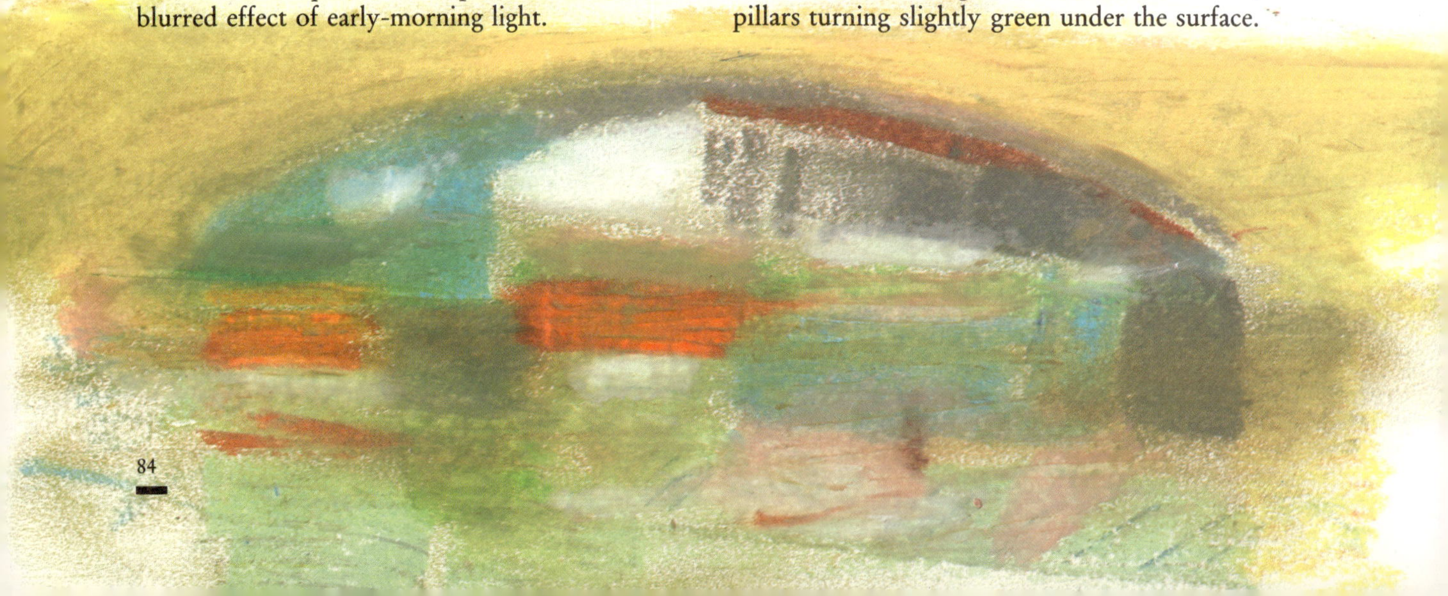

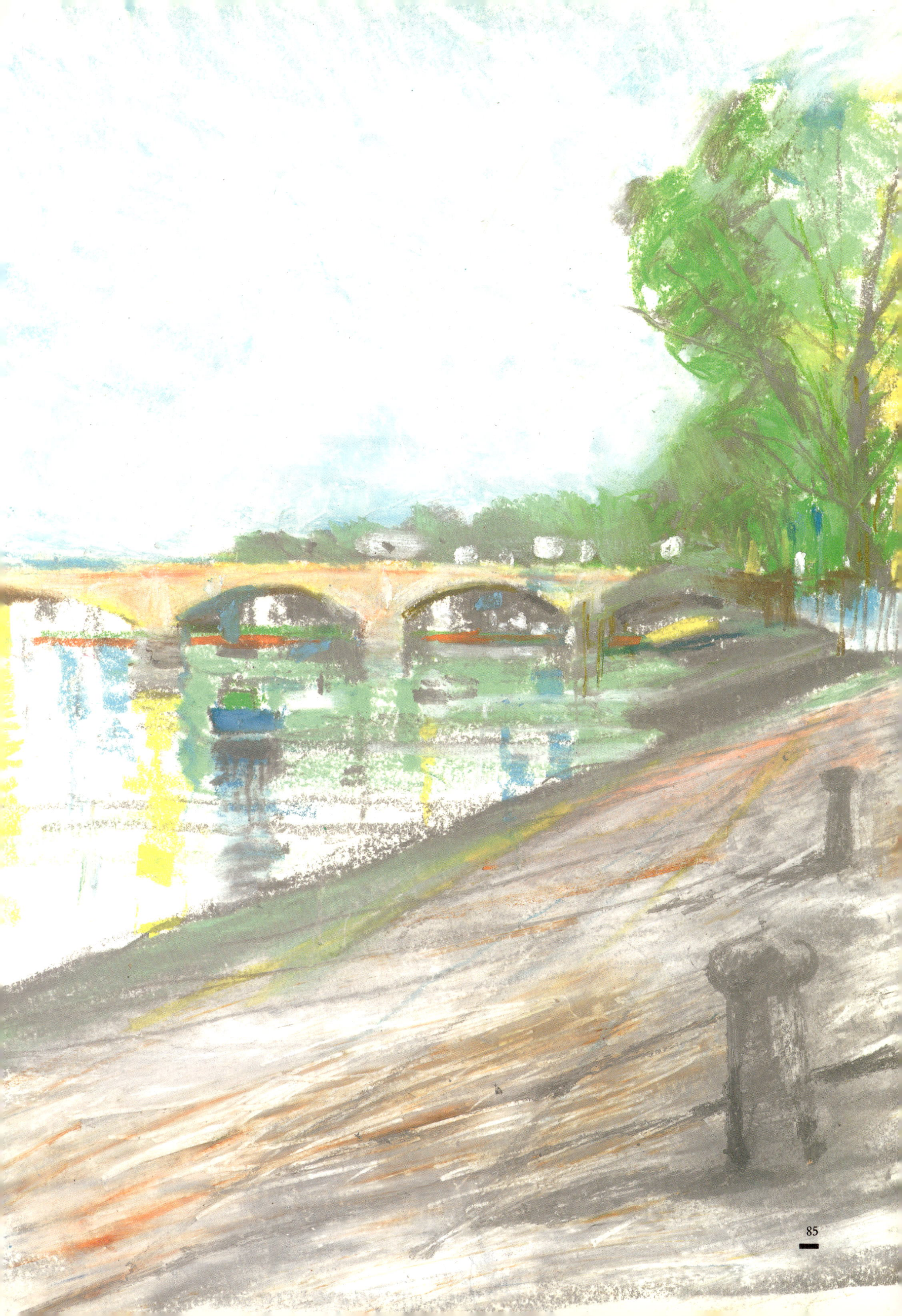

Red Fruit

Everything about this project revolves around the confident use of colour to make a fierce impact; the composition is built up on the base of one part of the spectrum, the objects are chosen because of their colour, and the focus is a cluster of shapes in the deepest colour of all. This is really seeing red!

I have been bowled over by the depth of intensity of oil pastels, and here that is exploited to its fullest extent. I could have used all blues and greens, but there is something so hugely attractive about clashing purples and oranges that the colours took over.

Make your setting with scraps of fabric, a few pieces of fruit, and so on. Although it is easier to work from reality, once you have the image you want fixed in your mind, then you can add in anything that you may not have to hand. The glass was actually dark green, but painting it yellow made a much more effective link with the other primaries.

The white bowls were deliberately placed to make the reds seem even redder. Leaving the paper white would not have made an equal impact. Matt paper would have faded under the competition, while the glossy white shines out like a beacon.

The drawing in this project is quite simple; the shapes are modelled with toning colour, the shadows are red mixed with brown. The light comes fairly high and from the side – to my mind, that is the best way to create highlight in any picture.

Above all, I hope that having the confidence to work with such strongly related colours should give you, too, a terrific lift. Pin the finished drawing up as your graduating exercise. I guarantee you will notice it every time you come into the room, for ever!

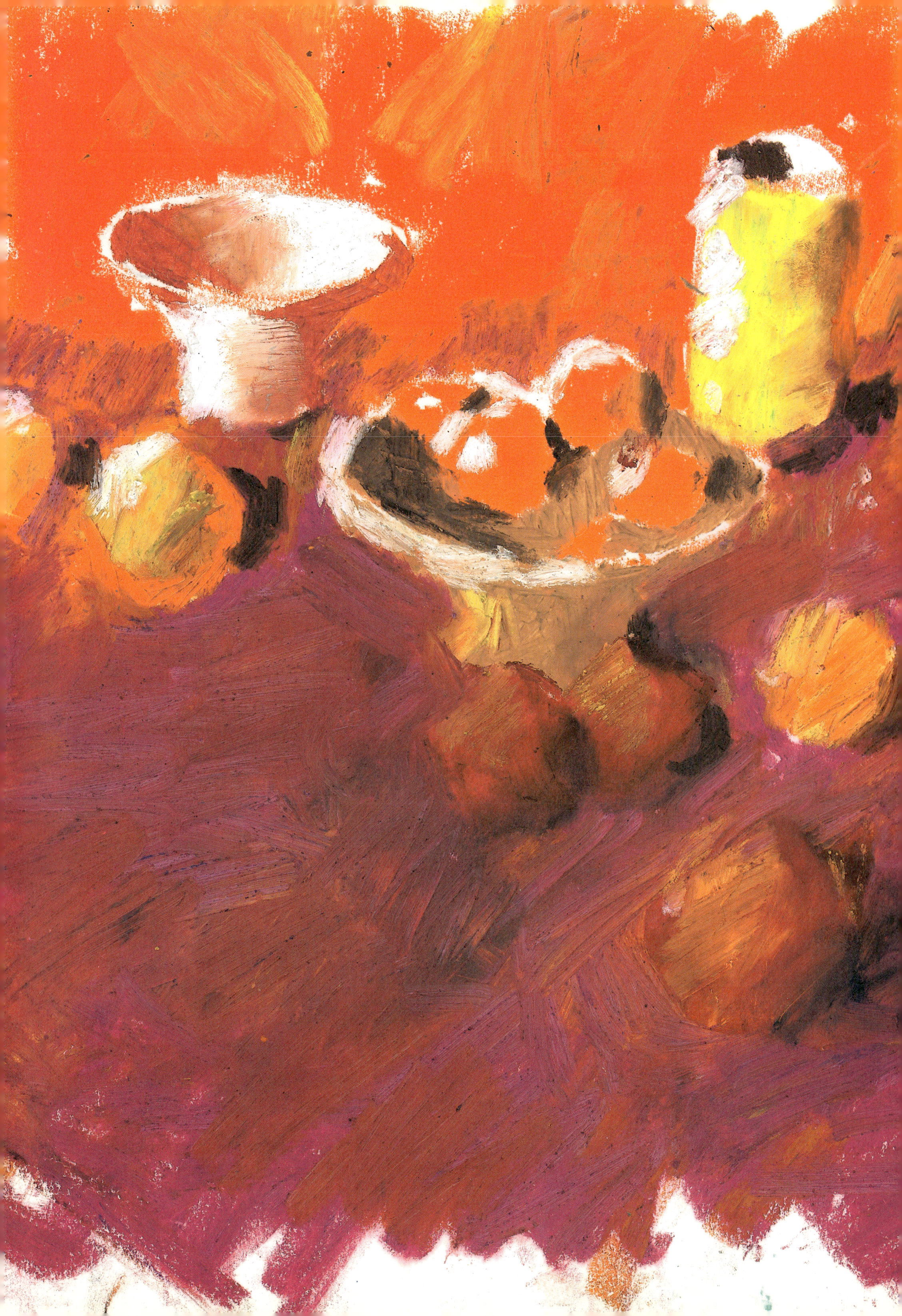

Pastel as a Medium

Soft Pastels

It is the purity of the colour that makes soft pastel drawings, even those 200 or more years old, look as fresh as if they were painted yesterday. Their contemporary oil paintings will have darkened, yellowed and cracked, and watercolours, unless protected within closed portfolios, will have faded.

All artists' colours have the same pigment; the difference between them is in the medium used to carry the pigment. Oil-based paint changes colour, loses its gloss and dries out. In watercolour there is so much dilution that what is left is the thinnest touch of pigment and a great deal of water, making the paintings very vulnerable to light.

But pastels are almost pure pigment. The chalk is used only as a filler and the quantity of gum is only enough to hold the stick together. The result is tiny flecks of colour that are caught in the surface of the paper as you work. These remain exactly as they are, so that this extraordinary medium, so apparently light and fragile, is actually the most permanent form of art.

Soft is the word we use for a stick mixed traditionally with precipitated chalk and little else. In fact, it is made in three different degrees: soft, medium and hard. Generally speaking, only soft and hard sticks are easily available. The firmness of the hard stick is due to additional gum; it makes a thinner, stronger stick, which can be more easily sharpened to give a crisp line. But some of the texture is inherent in the pigment; for example, ground earth colours are naturally soft, while malachite is naturally hard.

Making your own soft sticks is quite easy, and it is certainly worth trying once or twice. A formula is given on p. 89, and although an exercise in economy, it should also give an insight into how different textures are produced.

Making at least one batch of your own sticks will help to establish the texture that you feel is most responsive to your own individual style. Then it is a question of finding a similar commercial brand, and perhaps continuing to make just a few particular colours for yourself.

Some soft pastel colours are also available as pencils, encased in wood. Although these are extemely useful for keeping in your pocket while sketching outdoors – and, of course, for keeping your hands clean – they are not very adaptable. You can't make side-strokes or gradations of colour, and their range is limited.

The one cause of damage to a pastel drawing is touch. The Care and Maintenance Guide on p. 91 gives advice and information on how to avoid this by using a light fixative and simple mounts.

Pastels have another unique quality among artists' mediums; you cannot mix the colours. You can blend them, of course, but that creates a smooth surface which may not give the required effect. And of course you can create complex patterns, with overdrawn lines and hatches that create the illusion of a new colour. However, if you want to make a crisp, open-textured line in a particular shade of light green, you have to use a stick in that colour.

So there is no possibility of creating a simple palette with which you can, in turn, create all the colours you need. This is the one and only art form in which the more colours you buy, the better! And 'more' is the operative word; even beginner's sets usually have a minimum of twenty-four or thirty colours, and for the ambitious artist, the largest range I know of has 552 different colours, each available in individual sticks.

I have to admit that I have never owned a complete set of all 552, but any working artist is likely to try out well over 100, though only two or three dozen will always be in my box.

Making Soft Pastels at Home

All the ingredients will be easily available at any art supply shop. The only special equipment you need, if you want to make evenly sized sticks, is some sort of moulding apparatus; I've used an icing syringe, intended for cake decorating, with a fairly wide, simple, round piping nozzle. However, hand-rolled sticks are perfectly satisfactory for this experiment.

Ingredients

Gum tragacanth
Precipated chalk (some artists prefer to use either part or all talc, instead of chalk – they think it gives a more slippery feel and is easier to work. I don't, but try it for yourself!)
Dry pigments, in any required colour
Small amount of household disinfectant

Equipment

Mortar and pestle, or a good-quality small mixing bowl in pottery or plastic (not metal) and a strong wooden spoon
Spatula
Clean surface, such as a slab of pottery or a plastic-coated chopping board (not wood)
3 well-washed jam jars with corks or tight-fitting lids
Small scale for weighing, and a glass measure for liquids.

Method

Dissolve ⅓ oz (9.5 gm) of the gum tragacanth in 1 pint (600 mL) of warm water. Let it stand overnight in a warm place. You will get a kind of jelly; mix in a few drops of the disinfectant to keep it from spoiling or growing mould.

Divide the jelly into three and put each third into separate jars. Label them 1, 2 and 3.

Number 1 is the full-strength gum. Add an equal amount of water to Number 2 and mix well. This is the medium solution. Add twice as much water to Number 3. This is the weakest solution. Begin by using this diluted gum first, as the less gum you use the better. There is no precise way of telling you exactly which solution to use, or how much. Keep a record each time you mix a batch, because the results will vary depending on the humidity, the quality of the materials and their freshness. You may want to alter future mixes, and the records will be invaluable.

Begin by making white pastel: weigh out 2 oz (57 gm) of the chalk on to the slab and add about ½ fl. oz (15 mL) of gum solution Number 3. Mix well with the spatula until it is as smooth as stiff putty. If it is too dry, add more water; if it is too watery, add more chalk.

Put the putty on a newspaper, and roll with your hands into thin or thick sticks. For a more professional appearance you can use an icing syringe, as I do. Let the sticks dry in a warm place. When firm, cut into convenient lengths, and then continue to let them dry. The sticks should be left at least overnight in a warm (but not hot) place.

When you want the darkest possible colours, begin by grinding pure pigment in the mortar with sufficient Number 2 solution to make a similar putty, then mould as above.

For lighter tints, make up more pure pigment putty, mixed only with the smallest amount of Number 2 gum solution, then divide the result in half. Take one half and add an equal amount of white chalk putty as described above. Blend together thoroughly, then roll and dry.

Take the second half of the colour mix, divide that in half, and mix one half with twice as much chalk putty, and the other half with three times as much chalk putty. Each result will be less and less intense in colour.

You can keep going until you have only a smidgen of colour. But do remember to make sure that each mixture is thoroughly blended or you will have streaks when you start to work.

Oil Pastels

These fairly thick sticks are made with either oil or wax (or both) as an addition to the pigment; their characteristic mark is more or less sticky, depending on the brand and type. Although many of the techniques for using them are the same, the result will be very different in appearance from soft-stick pastels.

Oil pastels give the same effect as particularly rich, old-fashioned wax crayons, or as if the artist were working in oil paint, using a very dry, stiff bristle brush.

Oil pastels are relatively new, and so their permanence has not yet been established; in the long term they may suffer more from drying and from sinking colour than the soft pastels.

The range of colours is also much smaller, perhaps sixty or so, although this is constantly being expanded by new specialist ranges with multiple tints of black to white, iridescence and metallic glitter, as well as fluorescents, which are, as far as I am concerned, suitable mainly for painting socks and making children's murals. Such novelties are intended especially for graphic artists and designers and, as such, are a valuable resource.

One advantage of oil pastels is that they do not need fixing. Just let them dry properly, which (like oil painting) can mean at least overnight, and probably for days, possibly even weeks. They can even be varnished later if the colour 'sinks' into the paper too much.

Some painters have advocated the use of both oil and soft pastels, in the same drawing. After many experiments and after viewing other artists' work, I feel that the elements end up fighting each other. I prefer to let their very different qualities shine through on their own.

Oil pastels are harder to produce than soft pastels, so they are not really suitable for home manufacture.

Papers

Making a Paper Notebook

A special delight in working with pastel is that there are so many different kinds of paper that are suitable. Almost any drawing or painting stock can be used. However, the outer limits of the texture spectrum do cause problems: very smooth surfaces have no 'tooth' and so the chalks slide off without being able to make those characteristic, open-spaced marks. With very rough paper, the texture has definite peaks and troughs. The chalk catches the peaks, your hand gets constantly slowed down, and the marks skim the surface without making much contact.

But between these extremes, anything goes. Cartridge paper, drawing paper, tinted Ingres paper, brown wrapping paper (matt, not shiny), even sanding paper have all been used to great effect. Fabric can also be adapted by stretching it firmly over card or wallboard. Canvas with a smooth finish is very acceptable, and old-fashioned parchment or vellum is wonderful for light and delicate work.

To make a guide for yourself that shows how the choice of paper affects your drawing, start a 'notebook' by cutting a similar-sized sheet from every colour or different paper texture that you can find.

Take one stick of pastel and draw a thin line and then a side-stroke across the top of each example. Make a note of what that colour or tint is. Then take a second stick and do the same. Work down the paper with as many different colours as you can get on the one sheet. If you are really intrigued by what you see, as I was, put together a second set of the same papers and continue with new pastel colours. Eventually you will have a permanent guide to what each colour in your box will look like on a wide variety of papers.

You will be amazed how varied the results are. While I was drawing for this book I had the sheets pinned up on the wall as a working study. The shifting colours made an abstract picture of considerable charm.

Care and Maintenance Guide

Fixatives

As the experts seem to have proven with their historical examples, pastel drawings, even without fixative, survive better than almost any other form of paper art. However, this assumes that they have been protected from being rubbed continually while in storage, or from casual fingering as the drawings are taken out and re-packed.

Most of us have to make do with less ideal conditions. The first law is to fix your finished work as quickly as possible to avoid any danger of damage. In the past, much written advice was cautious about using fixative at all. Not unreasonably, because the older cellulose mixtures were unpleasant and smelly. Modern acrylic fixatives are lighter, with better sprays, and have no smell at all.

None the less, it should still be a case of minimum use. Spray from a distance of half a yard (or metre) and spray in light, short, whooshy bursts across the picture, stopping the spray at the end of each sweep to minimize the number of acrylic droplets falling in the air.

Your drawing will be dry in seconds and, by rubbing very lightly on a corner or an edge, you will be able to satisfy yourself that the fixative has worked.

Mounts

If you want to display your drawing, a quickly made mount is the best simple protection, and it adds to the impact of the finished work. There is the added convenience of covering up the rather messy edge, where the strokes are liable to have smudged and the paper gets dirtied by your working hand and arm.

Use a lightweight mounting board, available in any art store. Cut out a piece slightly bigger all round than your drawing. Using a sharp knife cut out the centre, taking away a piece smaller than your drawing, and leaving you with a simple frame. Put the frame face-down, lay the drawing upside-down on top and secure the edges with a little masking-tape.

This way almost everything you do can be pinned up while you decide whether it pleases you or not, and it will be well protected as well as looking that much better.

Storage

Once the pictures are ready to be stored, you can leave them in the frames for added protection, and put them in a pile face-down, with a piece of acid-free tissue between each drawing. Try to make sure the pile is kept tidy so that it won't break up and let the individual sheets be rubbed or damaged. You can make the pile secure with a few long strips of masking-tape, and put the whole thing into a large plastic bag.

The sticks of pastels should also be kept neat and tidy. The soft sticks are not as fragile as they look, but a box of them can create a lot of dust. Pastels usually come wrapped in paper and packed in boxes with separate individual compartments.

If you are buying new colours as separate sticks, make sure that you have enough space in your box, or buy an extra box or a second-hand cigarette case. The ones with elastic bands are perfect for holding the sticks in place.

The thinner sticks seldom have paper wrappers, so you can make your own with strips of tissue-paper. The wraps protect your hands when in use, and the sticks from rubbing or damage in the box.

If you have been using oil pastels in heavy concentrations, as you would in scratching and scraping techniques, for example, the oil binder may saturate the paper and bleed through to the other side, staining the drawing beneath. Take special care in such cases, and interleave the drawings with at least one sheet of acid-free tissue. Check the pile regularly to see that the staining has not run through the sheets.

One warning on your own care and maintenance! My hands are always getting multicoloured, as I manipulate the sticks and bits of compressed oil pastel with my fingers. Working in pastels requires constant reminders to keep your hands clean.

Shopping Guide

Buying pastels becomes a question of trying out different brands. Unlike oil and watercolour pigments, there are genuine differences between manufacturers' products – differences in the degree of hardness or softness, in the texture of the pastels on the paper, and particularly in the range of colours readily available.

Traditional soft pastel sticks are sold in sets of varying size, from about ten colours upwards. You can also buy them individually, but you will need some sort of solidly made box to keep them safe from accidental breakage. So once you decide which kind you prefer, it is worth buying one largish set and replacing the sticks when you need to.

Any good art shop will have some sticks for you to try. One brand may be so lightly pressed that they crumble as you work, while another's 'soft'-textured sticks may be more powdery, though just as soft. You will find that these are best for long sweeps, texture and for blending very easily. The French and Dutch brands are usually quite soft, and break up fairly easily.

Some 'soft' sticks are actually quite hard; you will need to use more pressure, and blending might be just a little more difficult. Ask the advice of your shop. It is worth investing in a few sticks of different makes, and trying them out for a few days on a variety of simple drawings and papers, before you purchase a large selection.

Beginner's boxes usually contain between twenty-four and thirty colours, which sounds generous but is really very limited. However, they are very useful as travelling boxes.

There are 'specialist' ranges for landscapes and portraits, but these are even more limited, being someone else's idea of what colours you need. I think they inhibit choice and restrict your imagination, particularly when part of the fun of using pastels is finding wonderful rainbows of colour in the shop, just begging to be used.

A fairly new product, available in Europe and America, is soft pastel in a wooden case, looking just like a largish pencil. The wood certainly protects the stick, makes it easier and cleaner to hold, easier to sharpen, and it is perfect for popping in your pocket on a sketching trip. But the range of colours is still quite limited, and more importantly, perhaps, the pastel 'lead' can be used only for thin-lined drawing rather than for 'painting' with side-strokes, for wider areas of background, and so on.

The use of fixatives has already been described. In buying your supplies, remember that some brands are not intended to fix the pastel as permanently as others. Some contemporary artists and teachers like to use this light fixative while they work, to keep the stages of each picture in place. Other products are designed for permanent fixing, so that the drawing remains undamaged on the wall or in the frame, and these are the ones I use myself.

My personal preferences do not include fixing work in progress. I think it stops you from the best part of the creative process – changes of texture or emphasis, which can and do occur continually as you work. In any case, I prefer to draw on the paper, not on a layer of fixative.

But you will have to try the various brands to see which is best suited to your own preferences. The labels don't offer much guidance, and so it's trial-and-error time.

Glossary

Binder, or binding agents:
Any substance that holds pigment together and helps it to adhere to a surface. In pastel, the binding agent is usually gum, but it may also be oil, wax, glycerine or even honey.

Blending:
The technique used to create a new colour from two or more different colours. In pastel, this involves rubbing on the surface of the paper until the colours run together. Because pastels cannot easily be blended, except directly on the paper itself, the manufacturers make eight tones to each colour, so that you can almost always find the colour you want without blending.

Blending is also the technique that burnishes the surface, by gentle, circular rubbing, so that the pastels are pressed into the paper to create an extremely fine, smooth layer.

Chalk:
Chalk is simply soft, powdered limestone, which, when pressed into shape with a little gum, creates a drawing stick of white colour. Chalk is also used as a filler for pastel sticks.

Charcoal:
Sticks of charred wood, the finest being of willow. The wood is charred in an oven, so that there is no air and the wood turns to charcoal, rather than ash, and is capable of being sliced into thin sticks. Boxes of charcoal come as thin twigs, which are best for fine drawing. There are also many larger sizes, which are used for sweeps and rich shadows.

Crayon:
Usually a wax-based stick used by children, but the term can refer to any drawing material in stick form, such as charcoal, chalk or pastel. There are now some experimental sticks of wax-based pastels, which are called pastel crayons.

Cross-hatching:
Using patterns of parallel, criss-crossing lines to create tones. Tiny cross-hatching, using the hardest soft pastels, will make very subtle shadows. The technique is not suitable for oil pastels.

Feathering:
The technique of letting the pastel lift off the paper at the end of a stroke, and then brushing the pigment with a tissue or a cotton-tipped stick, so that it disappears gradually from the surface.

Fixative:
Any liquid containing a binding agent suspended in a spirit, which is atomized and sprayed on to the finished pastel drawing. It inhibits the loss of dust or flaking from the surface, without changing the colour of the pigment too much. It serves the same purpose as varnishing in oil painting.

Focal point:
A small area of the drawing or painting that attracts the eye to it, either because of its placement and importance on the page, or because of the use of a brilliant colour against a soft or dark background.

Framing:
It is often very difficult when you are working outside to separate the part of the scene you want to draw from its surroundings. Make a couple of small cardboard frames for yourself – one square, one rectangular. They should have holes of roughly 2×2 inches (5×5 cm) and 2×3 inches (5×8 cm). Once painted black, they will give you handy portable viewfinders. Hold one out at eye level, close one eye, and move the frame around until the scene you want to draw fits inside it. If you are going to be working on the same picture at home, then take a quick snapshot, and use the frame to isolate your chosen subject. You will have a handy record for details that you might forget. A frame also comes in useful when you are isolating part of a room before you start drawing.

Highlight:
The lightest part of an object, often a reflection of natural light on a polished surface. Highlights are generally indicated by a tiny white square, or a white line. Sometimes yellow is used, to imply direct sunlight or lamplight, rather than daylight.

Local colour:
The actual colour of an object (in so far as the human eye is concerned), unmodified by distance or reflection. Thus a distant hill will have a local colour of green, even though from where you stand it might look blue.

Measuring:
An informal system for objects too large or too far away to be measured with a rule. It's based very simply on the practical use of your thumb or your pastel stick.

When you are ready to start drawing a group of buildings, look first at the largest individual building. Hold out your arm straight in front of you, holding your pastel so that it rises from your hand. Keeping your arm straight out, push the pastel up or down until the top of it seems to be at the same level as the top of the building. Then move your thumb until the tip of the nail is at the level of the bottom of the building. Bring your arm down, still keeping your thumb in place, and mark down the height of the building.

All the other buildings can be placed easily and quickly by relating them to that measurement. The neighbouring building may be only half as high, and so on. If it is a complex scene, check again by measuring one of the other buildings in the same way and seeing if it looks right on the paper. You can measure the height and width of almost everything this way – buildings, trees, etc. – and build up a pretty accurate framework for your drawing. Remember to keep your arm straight every time – that keeps the pastel the same distance from your eye, and gives you a standard scale to use.

Medium:
In art this has two meanings – the substance used to carry the colour (in oil paintings, linseed oil; in watercolour, water; in tempera, egg yolk; and in pastel, chalk), and the finished substance that the artist uses (so pastel is a medium with which the artist makes drawings and paintings). Chalk can also be a medium. If the term 'chalk drawing' is used, instead of 'pastel drawing', it usually refers to red- or white-chalk drawings.

Modelling:
The use of light and shade – which in pastel often means darker and lighter tones of the same colour – in order to give the illusion of three dimensions to an object, a form or a human figure.

Pastel:
An art medium, pressed into the form of a thinnish stick, which is used in the same way as a pencil or crayon. The most common association of the term refers to traditional pastels, now generally known as 'soft pastels'.

Pastel sticks are made from pigment, or powdered pure colour, a gum binder, and a filler that controls the strength of colour in the different tints.

Soft pastels are generally made in three degrees, ranging from hard (which behaves like a coloured pencil) through medium to soft. 'Soft' soft pastels have the most pigment and the least gum, so that their colour is the most brilliant of the three strengths, and they become so powdery that they create a colour surface much like paint.

Oil pastels are one of the newer variations in formulae, whereby the pigment is bound with oil rather than gum, and on the paper they look and behave much like oil paints. They can be thinned with turpentine and even applied with a brush.

Aside from their glossy surface, oil pastels have another advantage, in that they do not require fixing to be retained on the paper. However, because of the oil, the paper may become saturated and the colour may seep through the back, staining the pages beneath. *See* Care and Maintenance Guide.

The term 'pastel' also refers to the finished work executed in this medium, or to the technique.

Pointillism:
Literally, painting by dots (in French, *points*); the name given to the technique by the noted critic Félix Fénéon, when he first saw 'La Grande Jatte' (1886). This was the painting by Georges Seurat that established the technique and style, which were adapted by Seurat and Paul Signac especially. The intention was to use little dots or strokes of pure spectral colours together with white, and to lay them on the canvas in close proximity, so that, when viewed from a reasonable distance, the eye saw the

mixture of colours rather than the strokes. Most of the Impressionists experimented with pointillism from time to time, but only Seurat really regarded the technique as the finest possible tool for direct observation, and the creation of optical excitement.

Primary colours:
The three basic colours – red, blue and yellow – from which all other colours are made. *See also* Secondary colours and Tertiary colours.

Secondary colours:
The three primary colours combine to make three new, secondary colours – red and yellow to make orange; yellow and blue to make green; and blue and red to make purple.

Sgraffito:
The general term used for the technique of scratching a design through one surface, to a colour or layer beneath. Also used in painting, especially of early gold-leaf application, when a linear design was scratched through to the base.

Shading:
Blocks of tone used to create shadows.

Sienna:
Traditionally a red chalk, made from the iron-tinted earth found around Sienna, in Italy. There are red-earth deposits in many countries. Burnt sienna, as a colour, is made by heating the chalk to make a redder tint.

Tertiary colours:
These are made from mixing primary and secondary colours, although the tones become increasingly muddy and hard to keep separate on the palette. They are also increasingly difficult to describe. Blue and purple, for example, will make a bluey-purple; yellow and green a yellowy-green! It seems to be a very delicate balance, which varies from one person to another. I rarely talk about tertiary colours, but the term does get used in books from time to time.

Tint:
The lightening of a colour. When you add white or a plain filler to an original pigment to make a lighter tone, it is said to be a tint of the original. Pastels are the only medium in which you can buy tints ready-made – eight tints to a colour, in varying degrees of richness. In other painting mediums, you add white or water yourself, to create tints.

Tooth:
The degree of roughness of a paper – a paper with a smooth surface is called a fine-toothed paper; one with a very rough surface is called a coarse-toothed paper. Pastel should not be used on a polished paper, with little or no tooth, because it will simply slide right off, like drawing on a mirror.

Index

Many terms are used throughout the book; their entries in the index are restricted to particularly important notes, or to relevant sections in the text as well as definitions in the glossary. Individual projects are also listed, under the title of the finished painting. These are in italics.